Table of Contents

Descriptive Chemistry

Laboratory

Practice Examinations

Introduction

Welcome to the study guide! The Advanced Placement (AP) Chemistry Examination is designed to challenge a student's knowledge of the content of a college-level chemistry course.

This guide is not designed to replace an AP Chemistry course, but it will help you to review and prepare for the examination. If you have not taken the AP Chemistry course, you can use this guide as a general aid, supplemented with other materials like a college-level textbook. There is no specific or required curriculum for the course; however, there is a range of material typically included in a basic introductory college course on chemistry that will be on the examination.

Test Content

The test consists of 60 multiple-choice questions (MCQs), three long-response questions and four short-response questions in five different content areas:

1. Structure of Matter
2. States of Matter
3. Reactions
4. Descriptive Chemistry
5. Laboratory

Scoring

The test is scored on a scale of 1 to 5. A score of 5 means you are extremely well qualified to receive college credit, while a score of one means you are not qualified to receive college credit. While colleges and universities use scores differently, a score of 4-5 is equivalent to an A or B. A score of 3 is approximately similar to a C, while a score of 1-2 is comparable to a D or F. The examination is scored on a curve, and is adjusted for difficulty annually. This means that your test score (1-5) is equivalent to the same scores from tests in different years. The curve is different each year, depending upon the test.

Scores of 4 to 5 are widely accepted by colleges and universities; however, scores of 3 or lower may provide less credit or none at all. Elite schools may require a score of 5 for credit, and some schools vary the required score depending upon the department. You will need to review the AP policies at your college or university to better understand scoring requirements and credit offered.

Scoring on the multiple choice section of the examination is straightforward. You receive one point for each correct answer. There are no penalties for an incorrect answer or a skipped question. That means that if you are unsure, you should guess! Even the most random guess provides you a one in four chance of a point, while leaving a question blank guarantees you a zero. If you can narrow down the choices just a bit, your chances increase and, along with them, your possible test score.

The FRQs are scored from 1-8 depending upon the quality of the essay. Essay questions are graded by human graders, typically high school and college instructors who have been trained by the College Board.

Studying

This guide includes practice tests. While these tests familiarize you with the format and type of questions you will see on the test, they can also help you learn to employ your timing and test strategies and reduce your anxiety on test day.

Take the practice tests in a quiet, comfortable environment. Mimic the test environment as much as possible. Time the sections correctly and avoid getting up and down, fetching a drink, or having a snack. Plan to take the entire practice test in a single setting, just as you would on test day. Even if you can't do this for each of the practice tests, make time to do it for at least one of them, so you've had the full test experience once before the big day.

Staying Calm, Cool and Collected

Conquering test anxiety can help you succeed. Test anxiety is common and, if it's mild, can help keep you alert and on-task. If you're like most folks who get a little bit of anxiety, here are some tips to help you calm your nerves:

- Allow plenty of time for test preparation. Work slowly and methodically. Cramming doesn't help and will leave you depleted and exhausted.
- Remember to stay healthy. Sleep enough, eat right, and get regular exercise.

- Practice breathing exercises to use on test day to help with anxiety. Deep breathing is one of the easiest, fastest and most effective ways to reduce physical symptoms of anxiety.

While these strategies won't eliminate test anxiety, they can help you to reach exam day at your mental best, prepared to succeed.

The night before the test, just put away the books. More preparation isn't going to make a difference. Read something light, watch a favorite show, go for a relaxing walk and go to bed. Get up early enough in the morning to have a healthy breakfast. If you normally drink coffee, don't skip it, but if you don't regularly consume caffeine, today is not the day to start! It'll just make you jittery.

Make sure you allow plenty of time to reach the testing location and get your desk set up and ready before the examination starts.

Tips for Students with Serious Shakes

Some people don't find testing terribly anxiety-inducing. If that's you, feel free to skip this section. These tips and techniques are designed specifically for students who do struggle with serious test anxiety.

- *Control your breathing.* Taking short, fast breaths increases physical anxiety. Maintain a normal to slow breathing pattern.
- *Remember your test timing strategies.* Timing strategies can help provide you with confidence that you're staying on track.
- *Focus on one question at a time.* While you may become overwhelmed thinking about the entire test, a single question or a single passage often seems more manageable.
- *Get up and take a break.* While this should be avoided if at all possible, if you're feeling so anxious that you're concerned you will be sick, are dizzy or are feeling unwell, take a bathroom break or sharpen your pencil. Use this time to practice breathing exercises. Return to the test as soon as you're able.

What to Bring

- A sweatshirt or sweater, in case the testing room is cold.
- A bottle of water.
- At least two No. 2 pencils, sharpened.
- At least two black or blue ink pens.
- A wristwatch

And a quick note here: there's no need to take paper along. You'll receive not only the test booklet, but also additional scratch paper to take notes and make outlines for your free response questions.

All the best of luck to you on test day – now let's get started on the review!

The Structure of Matter

Units of Measurement

This section will provide a brief overview of common units used in chemical calculations and problems. Although you may already be familiar with these units, it can be useful to review them quickly.

Unit	Type	Value
Mol	Number	6.022×10^{23}
Gram, Kilogram, Ton (Tonne)	Mass	1 tonne = 1000 kg = 1,000,000 grams
Milliliter, Liter	Volume	1 liter = 1000 milliliters
Kilopascal, atmosphere	Pressure	1 atmosphere = 101.325 kPa
Cm, M, Km	Length	1 Km = 1000 M = 100,000 Cm
Joule	Energy	n/a
Coulomb	Charge	n/a

The most important unit here is the mol. One mol of a particular element equals that element's atomic mass in grams. For example, one mol of carbon weighs 12.011 grams. One mol of calcium weighs 40.078 grams.

The mol is a simplified method for understanding the numbers of atoms in relationship to the mass of a chemical, and is important in calculating solution concentration and reaction chemistry. This leads to a second important concept: that of molarity.

$$Molarity = \frac{mol}{liter}$$

The molarity of a solution tells us how many mols of an element are dissolved into a particular solvent, such as water, ethanol, or hexane.

Dimensional Analysis

Dimensional analysis is an important tool that can help you figure out whether out if you solved a problem correctly or not. The core principle of dimensional analysis is:

> *The scientific units of the numbers you are using to solve a problem should cancel out, such that the correct unit for the answer remains.*

Here is an example of how dimensional analysis can tell you that your answer is wrong: Let's say you are solving for mols. However, you get an answer of 25 mols/L. There is an extra L^{-1} in your answer. Is this answer correct? No!

When solving a problem, make sure to correctly display all the units in your work, so that you don't get lost. For example, here is the ideal gas law:

$$PV = nRT$$

In the ideal gas law, we have many different units. How can we make sure that we've solved a problem correctly? Let's say that our experiment involves a 20 liter container at 1 atm and 300 K. How many mols of gas are there?

$$n = \frac{PV}{RT} = \frac{1\ \cancel{atm}\ \times 20\ \cancel{L}}{0.08206\ \frac{\cancel{L} * \cancel{atm}}{mol * \cancel{K}} \times 300\ \cancel{K}} = 0.812\ mols$$

Because we wrote out all of the units and correctly canceled them out, we have arrived at an answer with the units (mols) as expected. This helps us confirm that our equation was correct.

The Elements & Atomic Structure

The basis of chemistry is the interaction of individual units of matter, called atoms. There are currently 118 discovered types of atoms, called the elements, and they are arranged in the periodic table. The study of chemistry is based on these elements and their individual properties. Many of the ideas behind chemistry are founded upon John Dalton's Atomic Theory, which states that:

1. An element is composed of atoms, which are extremely small, indivisible particles. Although we now know that atoms are composed of smaller units such as protons, electrons and neutrons, it is still recognized that atoms are the basic building block of matter.

2. Each individual element has a set of properties that are distinct and different from that of other elements.

3. Atoms cannot be created, destroyed, or transformed through physical changes. We now know that atoms can be created or destroyed, although this requires a massive amount of energy. Furthermore, radioactive elements can be transformed into other elements.

4. Compounds are defined by a specific ratio of atoms that are combined with one another, and the relative numbers and types of atoms are constant in any given compound.

Based on these rules, which were formed in 1808, the basis of modern chemistry was founded. Some of these rules have been disproved or modified since then. However, Dalton's understanding of atoms and compounds provided the information with which more elements and compounds were discovered, and their reactions with one another.

The Atom

The atom is the basic building block of materials and compounds. It is composed of a nucleus of protons and neutrons, surrounded by electrons, which form an electron shell around the nucleus.

The properties of the atom are largely determined by the number of protons and electrons. The number of neutrons will primarily decide whether or not the atom is radioactive.

- *Proton*: A proton is a positive charged subatomic particle with a mass of approximately 1.007 atomic mass units. The number of protons in an atom decides which element it is. For example, an element with 1 proton is hydrogen. An element with 12 protons is carbon.

- *Neutron*: A neutron is a non-charged subatomic particle with a mass of approximately 1.008 atomic mass units. The number of neutrons in an atom does not affect its chemical properties, but will influence its rate of radioactivity.

- *Electron*: An electron is a negatively charged subatomic particle with a mass of approximately 0.00055 atomic mass units. The number of electrons in an atom, in conjunction with the protons, affects the atoms surface charge. In addition, the number of electrons in the valence shell of an atom affects its reactivity.

Previous Models of the Atom

When the field of chemistry was young, many people proposed different models of how to represent the atom. It is important to understand these previous models, and even more important to understand the experiments which demonstrated that they were not correct.

Dalton's Model – Proposed: Early 1800's.

Dalton was the first to propose some aspects of atomic theory, including atomic weights and a general shape. According to Dalton's model of the atom, each atom was a single, indivisible unit that was solid. Simply put, an atom was something like a very small marble, and a solid was something composed of many of these marbles.

Dalton's model was disproved in the 1910's when the proton and neutron were discovered by Ernest Rutherford. Rutherford found that a hydrogen atom could be extracted from a nitrogen atom by collision, and that it had a positive charge. This showed that an atom was composed of smaller, positively charged pieces, and was not a single "whole."

Rutherford's Model (1911)

In Rutherford's model, it was proposed that an atom was a core of heavier particles, protons and neutrons, surrounded by a layer of electrons. In this model, the electrons were evenly dispersed around the core of the atom.

In Rutherford's model, because the electrons were evenly dispersed, classical descriptions of physics state that electrons will slowly lose energy while orbiting the nucleus. As a result, if Rutherford's model were true, all electrons would eventually collapse into the nucleus.

Bohr proposed that electrons can only orbit the nucleus in certain energy stages, or orbits, that are set distance from the nucleus. The electrons orbiting closer to the nucleus have the highest energy, and each shell of electrons expanding outward have a lower energy. He further proposed that it is possible to change the energy state of electrons through the emission or addition of electromagnetic waves.

Bohr's Theory

It is with Bohr's theory that the idea of electron shells was proposed, and Bohr's model is still used today, with some modifications, to understand the construction of the atom.

The conclusion (and the information you need to know for the exam) is:

"An atom is constructed of a core of neutrons and protons, and surrounded by various shells of electrons. The electrons maintain stable orbits around the nucleus of protons and neutrons, but can be excited to higher energy states."

The Atom

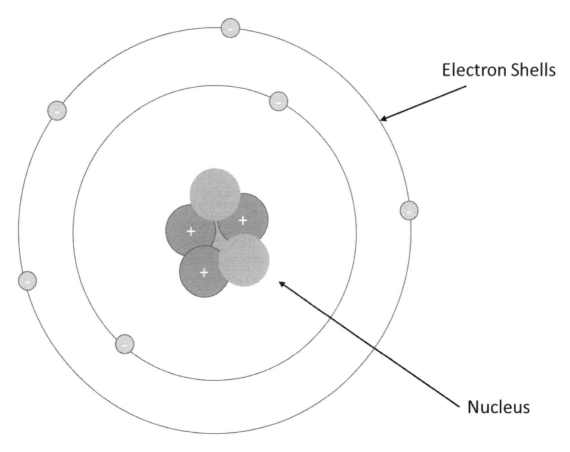

Electron Shells

Nucleus

Figure 1

The atom consists of a nucleus of protons and neutrons surrounded by a shell, or multiple shells, of electrons. The nucleus is very dense and contains the majority of mass in the atom. The actual size of the atom, due to the large electron shell, is much larger than the nucleus.

The reactivity of each individual atom is determined by the number of electrons in its electron shells, of which the most important is the valence shell. The valence shell is the outermost layer of electrons.

The valence shell configuration can be determined by looking at the periodic table (we'll cover that in a moment) and the shells of electrons have various names, summarized in the table below:

Shell	Electrons	Periods that contain it
S	2	Every shell
P	6	2nd period and greater
D	10	4th period and greater
F	14	6th period and greater

Looking at the periodic table, we come to understand the organization of these shells. The number of electrons in the outermost shells is represented by the column (group) and the number of shells is represented by the period.

For example, let's look at Iron (Fe). In the periodic table, iron is in the 4th period. That means that there are three shells of electrons, and one valence shell. The valence shell of the iron molecule will consist of 2 "S" shell electrons and 6 "D" shell electrons. The D shell has the capability of holding 10 electrons. That means that the valence shell of iron is not full, and iron is a relatively reactive element.

A special note is that although the majority of pictures show electrons in certain "orbits", a better description is that of an electron cloud. The exact location and orbit of an electron can be predicted, but according to the Heisenberg Uncertainty Principle, we can either know the position of an electron with certainty, but not the speed and momentum, and vice versa.

The two most important electron shells are the S-Shell and the P-shell. These electron shells are the outermost shells in the first three periods of elements (and in the later periods in groups 13 to 18), and form the reactive Valence Shell.

Shape of an S-shell

The S-shell orbital can contain 2 electrons, and is spherical in nature around the nucleus. Each period of the periodic table contains an additional S-shell layer. For example, Helium has a single S-shell, and when filled is termed as $1s^2$ (1st S-layer, with 2 electrons). Potassium has 4 S-shell layers, and the fourth S-shell is termed as $4s^1$ (4th S-layer, with 1 electron).

Shape of a P-shell

The P-shell can contain up to 6 electrons in three sets of orbits. The P-orbital is a figure eight orbital that occurs in three dimensions: x, y, and z.

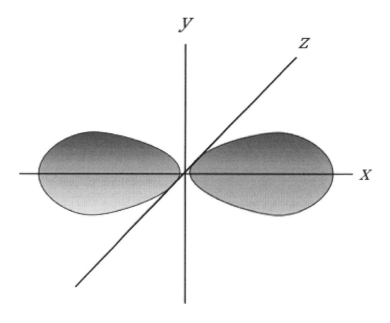

Figure 2

The figure above shows the Py orbital, or the P-orbital in the Y-direction. Each orbital (Px, Py, and Pz), can hold 2 electrons, or one pair. The naming of the P-shell for Oxygen is termed as $1p^4$, indicating the 1st P-shell with 4 electrons.

The valence shell for atoms in groups 13 to 18 is formed by the three P-orbitals. It is important to understand that the atoms in these groups can have between one and five bonds, depending on the P-orbital state. There are some exceptions to this rule that occur as the period increases, such as bonding with antimony (Sb) or Iodine (I).

Valence Shell Reactivity

The reactivity of a species depends on how many electrons are in its valence shell. Typically, the closer an atom is to reaching a 'full' valence shell, the more reactive it is. For this reason, elements in the first and 17th columns, which have one electron (one short of a full valence shell) are the most reactive. These elements, such as sodium, lithium, chlorine, and iodine, are extremely reactive.

There are some elements that are not very reactive at all. These are the noble gases, seen in group 18. The noble gases possess a full valence shell naturally. Thus, they have no free electrons with which to react. In chemistry, there are no common reactions that occur with a noble gas.

Introduction to the Periodic Table of Elements

The periodic table is a table used to organize and characterize the various elements, first proposed by Dimitri Mendeleev in 1869. A version of the periodic table is shown below. In the table, each column is called a 'group', and each row is called a 'period'.

Elements which share a column are similar in electron configuration, having similar numbers of electrons in their valence shell.

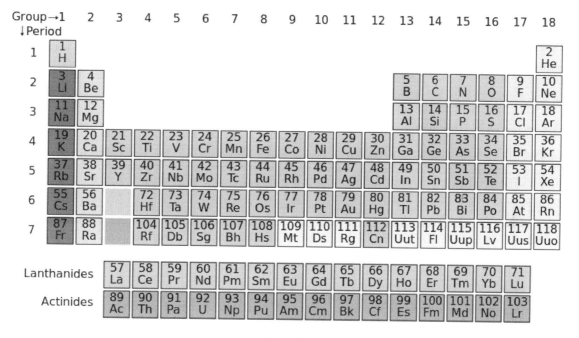

Figure 3

In addition, some element properties can be predicted based on the placement of the element on the periodic table. They are as follows:

1. Elements in groups 1 and 2 represent the alkali and the alkali earth metals, and are very reactive.

2. Elements in group 17 represent the halogens, and are very reactive.

3. Elements in group 18 represent the noble gases, and are very unreactive.

4. Elements along the "staircase" seen in gray in the periodic table above, consisting of Boron, Silicon, etc., are semi-metallic. They have some properties of metals, and some properties of non-metals.

5. The atomic radius of an element increases from the top left to the bottom right. The atomic radius is the smallest in the top left, and the largest in the bottom right.

6. The electronegativity of an element increases roughly from lower left to the top right. There are exceptions to this rule, and the noble gases are not included.

Reading the Periodic Table

In addition to the interpretation of chemical properties from the periodic table, additional information can be obtained for each element.

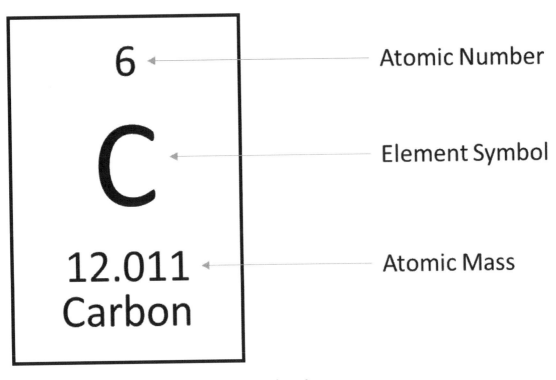

Figure 4

The number at the top in the table is the atomic number. This represents the number of protons the element possesses. The number below the element symbol is the atomic mass, which represents the total weight of the element (atomic mass – atomic number = # of neutrons.) In the example above, carbon has 6 neutrons.

The atomic mass is the weighted average of all possible species of the element. For this reason, it is almost never a whole number. For example, a small amount of carbon actually has an atomic mass of 13, possessing 7 neutrons instead of the usual 6. However, because the incidence rate of this form of carbon is less than 0.1%, it does not have a large effect on the average mass of carbon.

Properties of Elements

In this section, you'll find the properties of various groups of elements. You don't need to memorize all of the properties, but you should be able to recognize a group of elements and the rough similarities of the group's chemical properties.

Group 1 (The Alkali Metals)

The elements in group 1 are all silvery metals that are soft, and can be easily crushed or cut. They all possess a single valence electron, which makes them very reactive. The presence of just a single valence electron means that there is a high likelihood of losing the electron, resulting in a +1 charge for Alkali Metals. Because these metals are so reactive, they are not usually found in pure form. Bonds that involve Group 1 metals are always bonds that have high ionic character.

Group 2 (The Alkali Earth Metals)

The elements in group 2 are also silvery metals that are soft. These metals contain two valence electrons, which fill the S-shell, so these elements are not as reactive as those in group 1. However, they still have a high tendency to lose these electrons, and form a +2 charge. Normally, group 2 elements are found in this +2 oxidation state. Bonds that involve group 2 metals are almost always bonds that have high ionic character.

Groups 3 -12 (The Transition Metals)

The elements from groups 3 to 12 are called the transition metals, and are all capable of conducting electricity (some better than others). They are called transition metals in part due to their capability to possess multiple oxidation states. Due to the presence of the D-shell of electrons in these metals, they may have anywhere from a +1 to a +6 oxidation state, resulting in the formation of many different compounds and bonds. Transition metals are moderately reactive, malleable, and can conduct electricity due to the capability of gaining and losing many electrons in their outer electron shell.

Groups 13 & 14 (Semi-Metallic)

The elements in groups 13 and 14 are semi-metallic. They have moderate conductivity, and are very soft (such as aluminum). Elements in group 13 have three valence electrons and elements in group 14 have four, allowing for five and four bonds respectively.

Group 15 (Nitrogens)

This group is characterized by a shift from the top of this group (gases) to the bottom (semi-metallic.) This group has five valence electrons and can form three bonds. The semi-metallic elements, such as arsenic and antimony, are relatively reactive.

Group 16 (Oxygens)

This group is also characterized by a shift from the top of this group being gases and the bottom being semi-metallic. This group has six valence electrons and is quite reactive. The need to obtain only two more electrons to fill the valence shell means that these elements are all electronegative and typically possess a charge of -2. As a result, these elements are reactive and tend to bond with the alkali or alkali earth metals.

Group 17 (Halogens)

The halogens are all gases and all contain seven electrons in their valence shell. They are extremely reactive, much like the alkali metals. Due to their reactivity and gaseous form at room temperature, they are chemical hazards to humans. Inhaling chlorine or fluorine, for example, is usually deadly. The halogens will react in order to obtain a single additional electron to fill their valence shell and typically have a charge of -1.

Group 18 (The Noble Gases)

The noble gases already contain a full valence shell. Because their electron orbitals are already full, the noble gases are largely unreactive, except for a few rare exceptions. The heavier noble gases (xenon and radon) can sometimes react with other species under high temperature and pressure conditions. The noble gases have no net charge.

Metal Properties and Reactions

Here, we will examine some representative metals, such as iron, copper, and nickel, as well as some of their reactions. In addition, we will discuss the properties of metals and how these properties are related to the electron structure seen in the atom.

The "representative metals" are the metals that are first in each group on the periodic table. These metals are the most reactive in their group, and are quite common in nature. They include lithium, beryllium, manganese, iron, cobalt, nickel, and copper.

Group 1A (Alkali Metals)

The alkali metals are not found in their pure form in nature because they are very easily oxidized. Some pure forms can be produced in chemistry through electrolysis of salt forms, such as NaCl or KCl. Upon reaction with water or oxygen, these metals will immediately revert back to a salt (ionized) form.

The alkali metals have very low first ionization energies, which is the energy required to remove an electron from the atom. For example, lithium has a first ionization energy of just 520 kJ/mol. The further down the group we go, the lower the first ionization energy becomes. This low ionization energy means that an electron is very easily removed from the atom. When the electron is removed, the atom becomes ionized and gains a +1 charge. The formation of this charge and loss of this electron is the basis behind reactions involving elements in this group.

Example reactions of Group 1 metals:

$$4Li + O2 \rightarrow 2\ Li_2O$$

$$2Na + Cl_2 \rightarrow 2NaCl$$

Reactions involving group 1A metals are usually exothermic. This means that they release energy. In addition to releasing energy, the fact that the reaction is exothermic means that it is likely to occur spontaneously. If pure lithium is exposed to air, it will immediately oxidize and produce a flame.

The D-Transition Metals

The transition metals are those situated in the middle of the periodic table. They occur between groups 2 and 13. The definition of a d-Transition metal is one that has a d-electron orbital that is partially filled. All of the elements in this region share a set of properties, listed below:

1. All are metals. A metal is defined by the Oxford Dictionary of English[1] as "a solid material that is typically hard, shiny, malleable, fusible, and ductile, with good electrical and thermal conductivity."

2. Most of the elements in this region have high melting and boiling points and are solid at room temperature.

3. If a transition metal forms an ion or an ionic compound, it is usually colored.

4. Transition metals are able to form coordination complexes with ligands.

5. Transition metals are able to possess more than one oxidation state.

6. Transition metals are paramagnetic, meaning they can induce magnetic charges, or hold magnetic charges.

7. Many transition metals are effective catalysts due to their electron donating capabilities.

One of the most interesting properties of transition metals is their ability to have more than one oxidation state. Most of the transition metals are able to achieve a +2, +3, or +4 oxidation state. In the reaction below, chromium can have either a +2 or a +3 oxidation state:

$$Cr_2O_7{}^{2-} + 14H^+ + 6e^- \longrightarrow 2Cr^{3+} + 7H_2O$$

As a result, transition metals are able to participate in numerous different reactions that are not as predictable as the halogens or the alkali and alkali earth metals.

---

[1] http://www.oxforddictionaries.com/us/definition/american_english/metal

Coordination Compounds

A coordination compound is a metal complex that consists of a transition metal at the corn surrounded by a number of bound molecules or ions. The surrounding molecules or ions are known as ligands.

Similar to describing VSEPR geometry, a coordination compound is described by its coordination number (rather than a steric number) which refers to the number of ligands that are attached to the central metal atom. In most coordination compounds, the number of ligands attached can be easily counted, and number between 2 and 9.

Chemical Bonding

A chemical bond is a force that holds two atoms together. There are two primary types of forces: ionic and covalent.

Ionic Bonds

In an ionic bond, one atom has lost electrons to the other, which results in a positive charge on one atom, and a negative charge on the other atom. The bond is then a result of the electrostatic interaction between these positive and negative charges. In the example below, sodium has lost an electron to chlorine, resulting in a positive charge on sodium and a negative charge on chlorine.

Figure 5

Covalent Bonds

In a covalent bond, electrons are shared between two atoms. This can be in the form of one pair of shared electrons (a single bond), two pairs (a double bond), or three pairs of electrons shared (triple bond). In covalent bonds, one species has not lost an electron completely to the other. Seen below, the O_2 molecule is a double bond which results in the sharing of two pairs of electrons.

Figure 6

Note that there is a commonality between the two types of bonding. In both ionic and covalent bonding types, the bond results in each atom having <u>a full valence shell</u> of electrons. This is an important concept. Chemical bonding seeks to find the most stable electron configuration for all atoms involved. In the majority of cases, this means filling the valence shell of the atom either through the addition or removal of electrons.

Is It Ionic or Covalent?

How do you determine which bonds are covalent and which bonds are ionic?

This is a trick question, because bonds that exist between two different elements are a mixture of ionic and covalent. The only pure covalent bonds are those between two of the same element, such as O_2, N_2, or Cl_2.

All other bonds can be classified as having either primarily ionic character or primarily covalent character. A classic example of this is given below, in the interaction between hydrogen and oxygen in the water molecule.

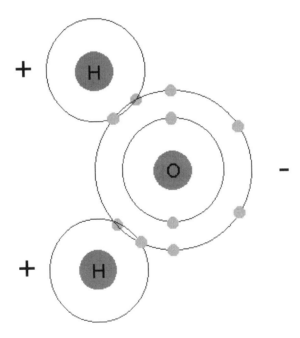

Figure 7

In the water molecule, there is a mostly ionic bond that exists between water and oxygen. The bond is considered to be mostly ionic if there is a large electronegativity difference between the two bonded molecules. In the case of water, the oxygen atom is much more electronegative than the hydrogen atom. As a result, oxygen pulls electrons

32

away from hydrogen. However, the electrons are still shared. In order to determine the nature of a bond, use the following guidelines:

- Is the electronegativity difference between the two atoms greater than 1? If so, the bond is mostly ionic. If not, the bond is mostly covalent.

- Are the two bonded atoms the same? If so, the electronegativity difference is 0. If the electronegativity difference is 0, then the bond is purely covalent.

Resonance Structures in Chemical Bonding

A resonance structure is a similar structural pattern for a molecule that has the same formula and types of bonds, but is slightly different in the placement of bonds or charges:

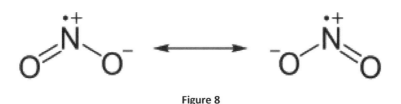

Figure 8

Intermolecular Forces

What causes water to stick together, forming a liquid at room temperature but a solid at lower temperatures? Why do we need more heat and energy to increase the temperature of water compared to other substances? The answer is intermolecular forces. Intermolecular forces are attractive or repulsive forces that occur between molecules.

There is a distinction between intra-molecular forces and inter-molecular forces and bonding. Intramolecular bonds are those that are seen inside of the molecule. The image on the next page shows an intramolecular bond.

Intramolecular Bond

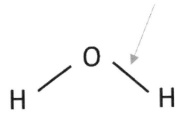

Figure 9

On the other hand, intermolecular forces occur between individual molecules, and are not bonds that actually connect atoms together. Below is a depiction of the intermolecular forces that hold water together.

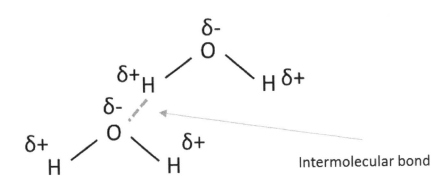

Intermolecular bond

Figure 10

Due to the electronegativity differences between oxygen and hydrogen, a dipole is created in the molecule, where oxygen has a slightly negative charge and hydrogen has a slightly positive charge. This charge difference forms a bond between molecules, or an intermolecular bonds.

The intramolecular bonds, such as the ionic or covalent bonds seen in CH_4 or NaCl, are 25 to 40 times stronger than any intermolecular force. For example, the bond strength of the covalent O-H bond is 464.5 kJ/mol, but the bond strength of the hydrogen bond holding water together is only 19 kJ/mol.

There are two main types of intermolecular forces that you need to know for the test: Dipole-dipole interactions, and Van der Waals forces.

Dipole-Dipole Interactions

A dipole is a separation of positive and negative charges that forms over the length of a bond. A dipole is created when one element in a bond has a significant difference in electronegativity compared to the other element in the bond. Examples of bonds that have strong dipoles would include C-O, O-H, or C-Cl. Examples of bonds that have weak dipoles would include N-N, C-N, or Fe-C. The method of determining the strength of the dipole is by looking at the electronegativity difference, which can be found in the table below.

```
Electronegativity increases ->
 Group   1   2    3   4    5   6    7   8    9   10   11  12   13   14  15  16   17  18
 Period

   1     H                                                                         He
         2.1                                                                        É

   2     Li  Be                                           B    C   N   O    F   Ne
         1.0 1.5                                          2.0 2.53.0 3.5 4.0 n/a

   3     Na  Mg                                           Al   Si  P   S    Cl  Ar
         0.9 1.2                                          1.5 1.82.1 2.5 3.0 n/a

   4     K   Ca  Sc Ti   V   Cr  Mn  Fe   Co  Ni  Cu  Zn  Ga  Ge  As  Se   Br  Kr
         0.8 1.01.3 1.5 1.6 1.61.5 1.8 1.9 1.81.9 1.6 1.6 1.82.0 2.4 2.8 n/a

   5     Rb  Sr  Y  Zr   Nb  Mo  Tc  Ru   Rh  Pd  Ag  Cd  In  Sn  Sb  Te   I   Xe
         0.8 1.01.2 1.4 1.6 1.81.9 2.2 2.2 2.21.9 1.7 1.7 1.81.9 2.1 2.5 n/a

   6     Cs  Ba  Lu Hf   Ta  W   Re  Os   Ir  Pt  Au  Hg  Tl  Pb  Bi  Po   At  Rn
         0.7 0.9     1.3 1.5 1.71.9 2.2 2.2 2.22.4 1.9 1.8 1.91.9 2.0 2.2 n/a
```

Figure 11

If we compare the electronegativity values in a bond, we can assume that a difference of greater than 1 will generate a significant dipole, and a difference of less than 1 will still have a dipole, but is unlikely to be one strong enough to cause significant intermolecular forces.

In some larger molecules, although an individual bond might have a dipole moment, the molecule at large will not have a dipole moment. For example, in a molecule such as the one seen on the next page...

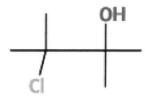

Figure 12

...although the C-Cl and C-OH bonds each have some bond polarity, the molecule itself does not have much of a dipole, because the negative dipoles on those individual bonds cancel each other out.

Van der Waals Forces

Van der Waals forces are the sum of small force interactions between molecules that are a result of forces that **are not** covalent, ionic, or hydrogen bonding in nature. Van der Waals forces include three types:

1. Keesom Forces
2. Debye Forces
3. London Dispersion Forces

Of these three forces, the most important to know for the exam is the London Dispersion Force, but you need some background on the other two, as well:

- *Keesom Forces* - named after Willem Keesom, these are attractions that occur as a result of rotation around a bond. Molecules are not static, and their bonds may rotate. As a result, small forces are generated due to new positioning of functional groups.

- *Debye Forces* - also known as induced dipole forces, Debye forces are weak forces that are induced by the presence of a stronger force on another molecule. For example, if the strong dipole on a water molecule induces a dipole force on a nearby ethanol molecule, it is a Debye force.

- *London Dispersion Forces* – these are commonly seen on non-polar molecules and occur due to the movement of electron in parallel. London dispersion forces become more significant as the atoms involved become larger. For example, bromine and iodine, the larger halogen elements, experience much more London forces compared to fluorine or chlorine.

Chemical Formulas and Naming Conventions

A chemical formula is a name that tells us the chemical composition of a compound or molecule. There are two methods that we can use to name a compound: the molecular formula, which is composed of the acronyms for each individual element, and the chemical name.

The chemical formula is based off of the individual element names. For example, oxygen is O, nitrogen is N, and calcium is Ca. Many of these elements are not found isolated in nature. For example, it is very unusual to find pure calcium. Instead, they are found in compounds mixed with other elements. One example of such a compound would be calcium oxide, or CaO.

A compound is defined as a mixture of a combination of elements in a defined ratio. A defined compound will always have the same ratio of elements. For example, calcium oxide is *always* CaO. It is never CaO_2 or CaO_3. If the ratio of elements in a compound changes, then the compound itself also changes.

Writing a Chemical Compound Formula

There are two methods for writing a chemical formula. The first is the simplest, and simply states the ratio of elements in a compound. For example, the compound acetic acid has the following formula:

$$C_2H_4O_2$$

This tells us that a single molecule of acetic acid has 2 carbons, 4 hydrogens, and 2 oxygen atoms. However, this chemical formula does not tell us much about the structure of the compound. In fact, it is difficult to understand from this formula how the structure of acetic acid might be acidic. For example, there are two structures on the next page – you decide which one is correct.

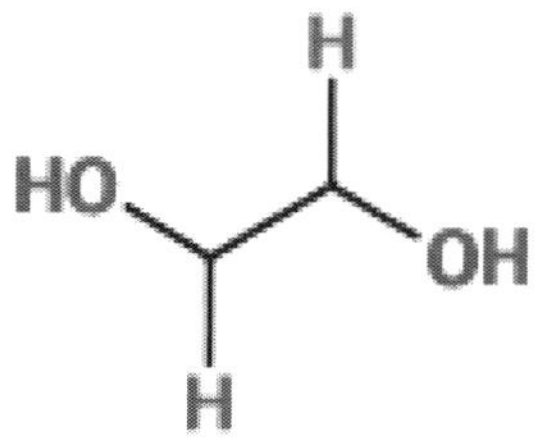

Figure 13

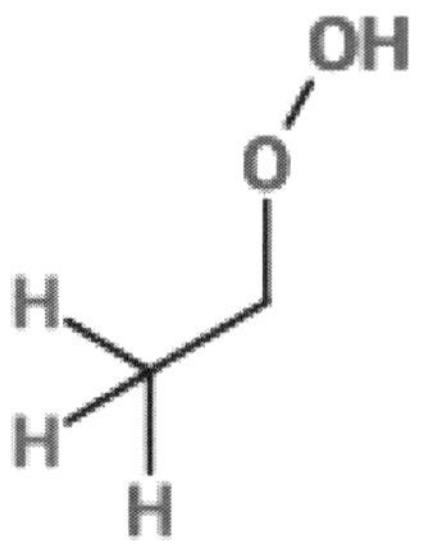

Figure 14

They both have the same chemical formula of $C_2H_4O_2$, but the structural properties are quite different. In the case of acetic acid, the correct structure is the one on the bottom. The carboxylic acid group of –COOH is what gives acetic acid its acidic properties. So how do we express that in a chemical formula? This leads us to the second method of writing a chemical formula: functional group notation - a specific group of elements that possesses consistent properties across all molecules (we'll cover this in detail a little later in the guide.)

When we write a chemical formula using functional group notation, we move the letters around in the formula to reflect the correct order of the elements in the compound. In this manner, we could write the chemical formula for acetic acid as:

$$CH_3COOH$$

This tells us that the first carbon in the molecule is attached to three hydrogen, and then to the next carbon, which is attached to the O-O-H chain. This gives us a better idea of the actual structure of the molecule. On the exam, you will likely see both forms of a chemical formula, the standard notation and the functional group notation.

40

Below is a table showing common chemicals and their standard formula as well as their functional group formula. Note that in some cases, the standard formula is the same as the functional group formula.

Name	Standard Formula	Functional Group
Hydrogen Peroxide	H_2O_2	HOOH
Acetone	C_3H_6O	CH_3COCH_3
Ethanol	C_2H_6O	CH_3CH_2OH
Benzene	C_6H_6	C_6H_6
Propane	C_3H_8	$CH_3CH_2CH_3$
Sulfuric Acid	H_2SO_4	H_2SO_4

Ionic Compound Nomenclature

Ionic compounds are formed from one or more cations (having a positive charge) and one or more anions (having a negative charge). The naming rules for ionic compounds are:

1. The cation is written first, followed by the anion. The cation has no suffix added. The anion has a suffix of –ide in the majority of cases (such as sodium chloride).

2. The stoichiometry of the molecule, as indicated by the subscripts, must produce a molecule that has no net charge. For example, $NaCl_2^-$, sodium dichloride, is not a valid compound.

3. The compound should be an empirical formula – it should have the lowest subscripts possible. For example Na_2Cl_2 is not correct.

4. A polyatomic anion, such as SO_4^{2-} does not have parentheses unless there are multiples of the anion. For example, $Na_2(SO_4)$ is not correct. However, $Al_2(SO_4)_3$ is a correct formula because there are 3 sulfate anions.

Based on these rules, we can name quite a few compounds. However, we need to know the names of common anions in order to produce the correct names! A table of common anions is on the next page:

41

Anion Name	Formula	Charge
Nitrate	$-NO_3$	-1
Sulfate	$-SO_4$	-2
Hydroxide	$-OH$	-1
Carbonate	$-CO_3$	-2
Phosphate	$-PO_4$	-3

Using this information, we can recognize the formulas of many common ionic compounds. On the test, it is expected that you can derive a chemical formula from the nomenclature of an ionic compound.

For example, we see in a problem that a student is using the chemical Potassium Phosphate. What is the chemical formula? First, we recognize that phosphate has a -3 charge. Then, we recognize that potassium, being an alkali metal, has a +1 charge. According to the naming rules, all ionic compounds must result in a neutral charge. Thus, there should be three potassium atoms in order to neutralize the -3 charge from the phosphate. The chemical formula should be:

$$K_3PO_4$$

Naming Covalent Compounds

The naming of covalent compounds is similar, with the exception that covalent compounds do not usually have cations or anions. In the naming of covalent compounds, the following rules apply:

1. The first element is named, along with a prefix indicating the stoichiometric value.

2. The second element is named, along with an appropriate suffix.

3. The first element, if having a value of 1, does not use the prefix mono-.

Here are some examples of covalent compounds with their full names:

Chemical Formula	Name
CH_4	Carbon tetrahydride
CO_2	Carbon dioxide

The prefix is based on the number of atoms present, and follows this convention:

Number	1	2	3	4	5	6	7	8	9
Prefix	Mono	Di	Tri	Tetra	Penta	Hexa	Hepta	Octa	Nona

Based on this information, we can derive the chemical formula from a name given for a covalent compound.

Functional Groups and Properties

Functional groups are a topic typically covered in organic chemistry. However, the knowledge of several common functional groups and their properties will greatly aid you in understanding chemical reactions.

Common Non-Polar groups

Methyl Group

The methyl group ($R-CH_3$) is a non-charged, stable functional group that is seen many compounds. All fuels have methyl groups, such as gasoline or diesel. The methyl group has very strong bonds between the carbon and hydrogen that is difficult to dissociate. As a result, the methyl group will not commonly react. Below are some examples of molecules that contain a methyl group:

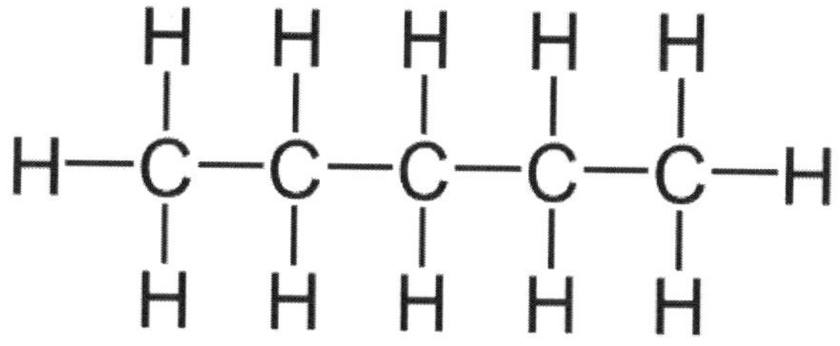

Figure 15

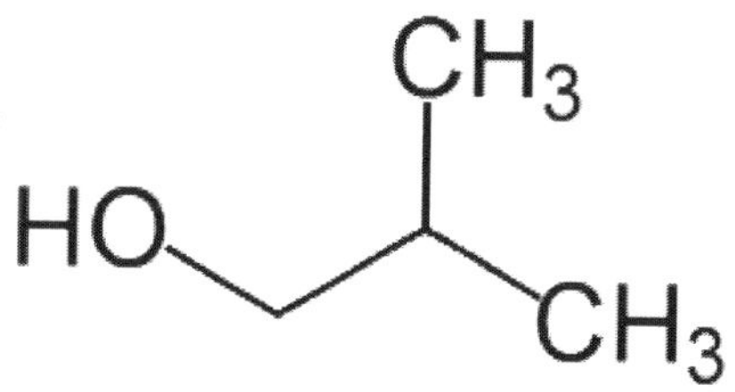

Figure 16

Benzene or Phenyl Group (R-C₆H₅)

The phenyl group is a non-charged, aromatic functional group that is very stable. The phenyl group is present in many larger molecules, including antioxidants and vitamins. You will likely not see this group much in the AP chemistry exam. Some examples of the phenyl group are seen below.

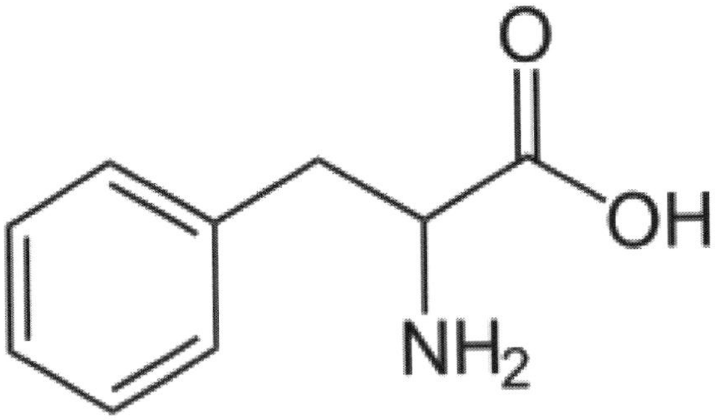

Figure 17

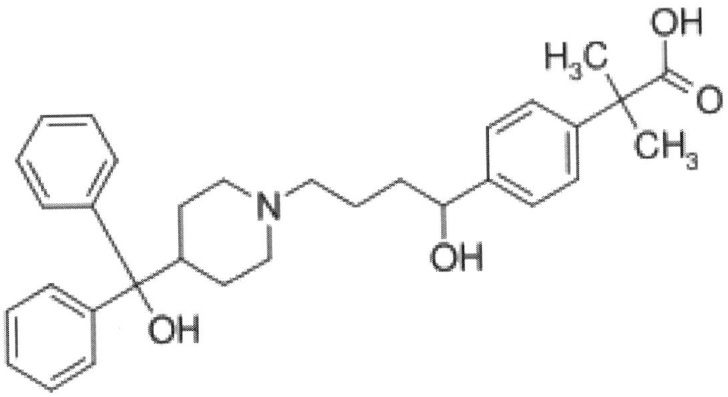

Figure 18

Common Acidic Functional Groups

Acidic functional groups are able to donate a proton. The AP exam will likely contain questions regarding common acidic functional groups.

Amine Group (-NH- or –NH₂)

The amine group contains a nitrogen atom bound to one or more hydrogen atoms. The amine group is able to donate a single proton or accept a basic group, in that manner acting as an acid. Amine groups are commonly seen in proteins. Some examples are on the next page:

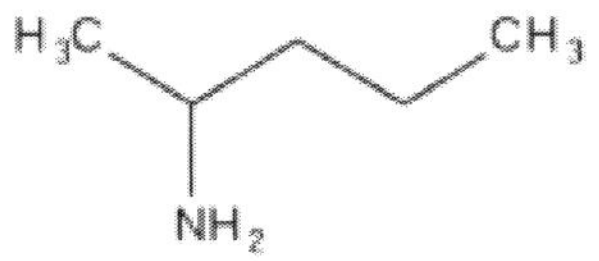

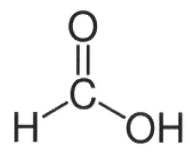

Figure 19

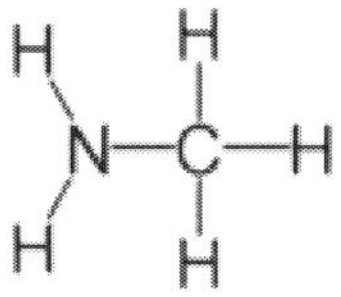

Figure 20

Carboxylic Acid (-COOH)

The carboxyl, or carboxyl acid group, is able to donate the single proton attached to the end of the oxygen to form an acid. Carboxyl groups are common in vinegar and amino acids, and some alcohols can be modified to contain a carboxylic acid. Some examples are below:

Figure 21

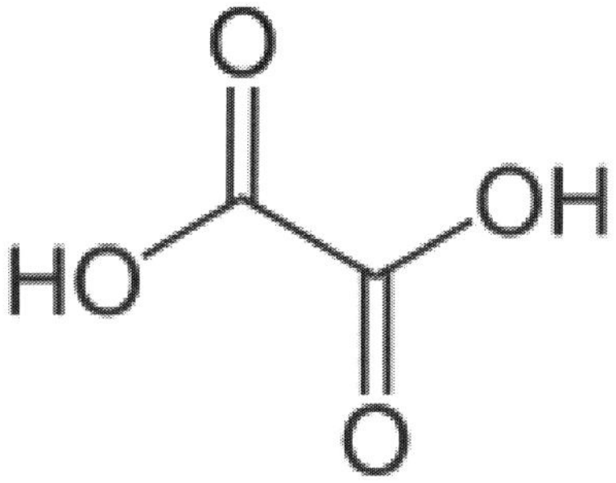

Figure 22

Basic Functional Groups

Basic functional groups are able to accept a proton, lowering the pH of a solution.

Nitrile (-CN)

The nitrile group consists of a carbon with a triple bond to nitrogen. The nitrogen atom is able to accept a proton and gain a positive charge. Some examples are shown below:

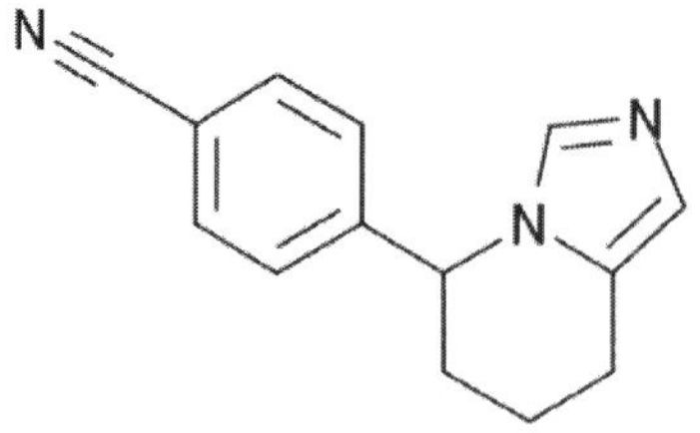

Figure 23

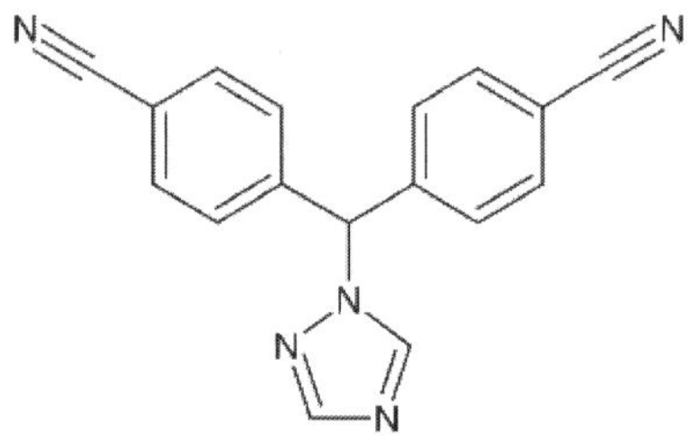

Figure 24

The knowledge of these functional groups will help you determine a particular reaction that might be occurring. In addition, given a general chemical formula, the understanding of the structure of these functional groups will help you write down a formula that has functional group notations.

Lewis Structures and VSEPR Theory

Lewis structures are diagrams used to represent the location of electrons in a bond. They are also called Lewis dot diagrams or electron dot diagrams. In these structural drawings, each dot represents a single electron. These structures can be drawn for bonds that are covalent in nature, meaning they share electrons. Ionic bonds are not usually represented using Lewis diagrams because there are no shared electrons.

In a Lewis dot diagram, the number of dots or electrons surrounding the atom is represented by the number of valence electrons that the atom has. For example, as seen below, oxygen has six valence electrons, carbon has four, and hydrogen has just one.

Figure 25

When drawing a Lewis dot diagram, the electrons are filled in one by one. As seen in the carbon molecule, there are no paired electrons, because carbon has only four electrons in its valence shell. For this reason, carbon is able to form four bonds. The hydrogen atom has just one free electron, and is able to share that electron to form a single bond. The oxygen atom has two free unpaired electrons, and is able to form two bonds. Drawing and examining Lewis dot diagrams is a useful tool that helps you understand the electron structure of the valence shell and how many electrons are required to fill the valence shell of a particular atom.

Valence Shell Electron Pair Repulsion (VSEPR) Theory

The VSEPR theory is used to predict the shape of molecules that contain two or more atoms. Electrons carry a negative charge, and as a result, will repel one another. For this reason, bonded atoms will form an arrangement that minimizes the repulsive forces to form a stable compound. This will form a particular geometry.

The geometry of a species is determined by several factors:

1. *Steric Number* – The steric number is the number of adjacent atoms attached to a central molecule. For example, the molecule CH_4 (methane) has a steric number of 4. It has four hydrogen atoms attached to one central carbon molecule.

2. *Lone Electron Pairs* – Lone electron pairs on a molecule will repel adjacent bonds, even though the electron pairs are not bonded to anything themselves. For example, in the molecule NH_3, nitrogen has a single pair of lone electrons. As a result, the shape of the molecule is changed.

3. *Electronegativity* – The electronegativity of a species will pull electrons away from other bonds in the molecule. As a result, although the core geometry may be the same, the bond angles between atoms will be different.

Common Types of VSEPR Geometries

Here, we will discuss the most common types of VSEPR geometries. On the exam, you will need to identify the geometry of a molecule based on its name and composition.

Steric # = 2

A linear molecule has a steric number of 2. It has a central atom attached to two other atoms. When no electronegativity forces are present, the bond angle is 180 degrees between each atom.

Figure 26

Steric # = 3

A steric number of three has either a trigonal planar shape or a bent shape, depending on if there is a lone pair of electrons present.

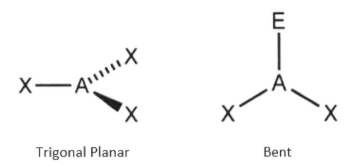

Trigonal Planar   Bent

Figure 27

The bent configuration possesses a lone pair depicted by the "E". The repulsion of the lone pair results in the atom shape being bent, although there is no bonding interaction.

Steric # = 4

A steric number of 4 involves many carbon molecules and nitrogen molecules, which have the possibility of binding to four species, including a lone pair.

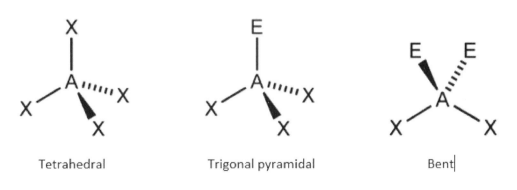

Tetrahedral   Trigonal pyramidal   Bent

Figure 28

The trigonal pyramidal and bent configurations possess one and two pairs of electrons, respectively. The bent configuration with a steric number of 4 represents the water molecule, with oxygen being the central atom having two pairs of free electrons.

Steric # = 5

A steric number of 5 has a single atom in the center with 5 surrounding bonds. In the figure below, the shape of the molecule depends on the number of free electron pairs that are in the molecule. The most common is that of the trigonal bipyrimidal, which has no free electron sets.

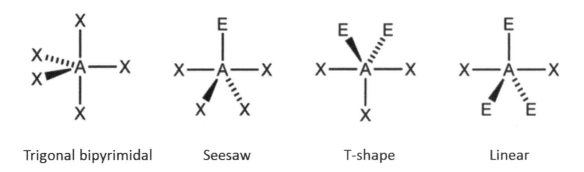

| Trigonal bipyrimidal | Seesaw | T-shape | Linear |

Figure 29

Steric # = 6

6 is the highest steric number that you are likely to see in common compounds. Examples of molecules with a steric number of 6 are SCl_6 (sulfur hexachloride), or XeF_4 (Xenon fluoride). These compounds are relatively uncommon. The geometries that are possible are seen below:

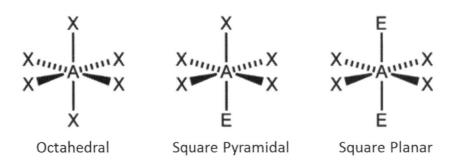

| Octahedral | Square Pyramidal | Square Planar |

Figure 30

The VSEPR geometries of some compounds are difficult to predict. These compounds include some transition metal compounds that are heavier, such as tungsten, platinum or gold. For these heavy transition metals, a different electron bonding theory prediction of bond structure, called VALBOND, is used. This topic will not be tested on the exam.

Some structures also exist with seven or eight bonds, but they are extremely rare and not applicable to most chemical reactions.

States of Matter

Structures and Properties of Molecules

The structure of a molecule greatly affects the properties of that molecule.

Boiling Point and Freezing Point

The boiling point and freezing point of a molecule are related to its structure. There are three important factors to consider when looking at a molecule:

1. *Strength of Intermolecular Forces.* The greater the intermolecular force, the greater the boiling point of the substance will be.

2. *Molecule Size.* As the molecule becomes larger, the boiling point of the molecule typically increases.

3. *Molecule Branching.* As more branch points are present in the molecule, the molecule's boiling point will increase.

Strength of Intermolecular Forces

A classic example of the differences in boiling point here is the difference between methane and water. Methane has a molecular weight of 16 g/mol, and water has a molecular weight of 18 g/mol. Neither molecule is branched. As a result, factors 2 and 3 (as listed above), are not relevant. Water has a boiling point of 100 °C. Methane has a boiling point of -164 °C. This is a huge difference!

The reason is because water is a highly polar molecule that has strong intermolecular forces. On the other hand, methane is an uncharged, non-polar molecule with next to no intermolecular forces. As a result, the energy required to break the bonds between water molecules, and cause the phase change from liquid to vapor, is much greater than that for the methane molecule.

Molecule Size

As the size of a molecule increases, the corresponding boiling point increases. This can be thought of simply as the energy required to 'loosen' a mess of large molecules. We can see this phenomenon in real life in hydrocarbon chains.

Name	Formula	Mass (g/mol)	Boiling Point (C)
Propane	C_3H_8	44.1	-42
Butane	C_4H_{10}	58.1	-1
Hexane	C_6H_{14}	86.1	68
Octane	C_8H_{18}	114.2	125
Decane	$C_{10}H_{22}$	142.3	174.1

In the table above, as the hydrocarbon length and corresponding mass increase, the boiling point also increases.

Molecule Branching

The last factor that can affect the boiling point is the shape of the molecule. Of the two molecules seen below, which do you think has the higher boiling point?

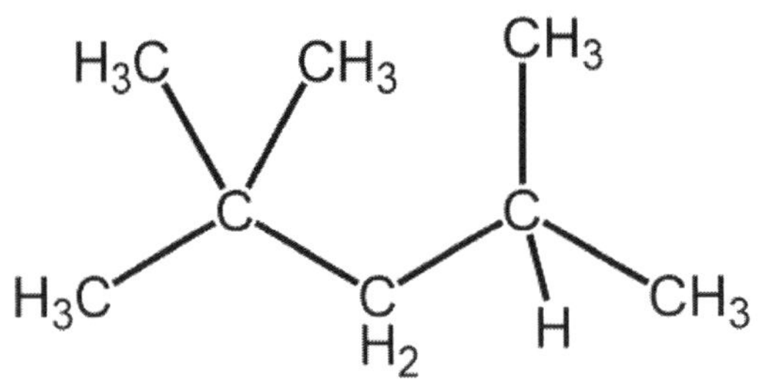

Figure 31

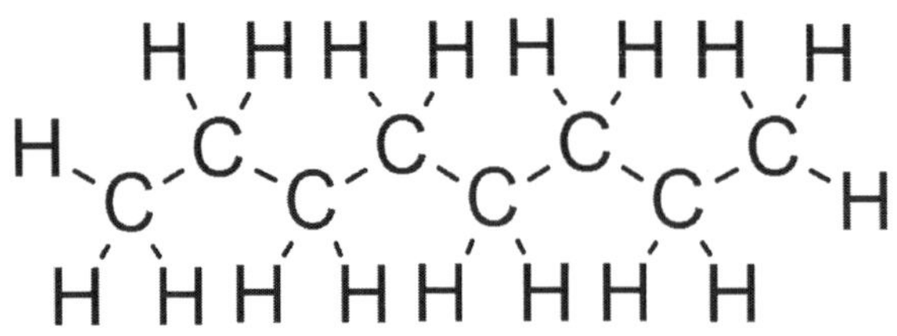

Figure 32

The structure on the bottom has the higher boiling point. It is called iso-octane, and has several branch points, whereas the structure on the right, octane, does not. The branch points and boiling point correlation can be difficult to understand sometimes.

In non-charged molecules, the presence of a branching points which make the molecule "smaller" will actually reduce the boiling point. In this case, isooctane has a boiling point of 99 C. In larger molecules that have polar groups, the branching of the molecule will increase the boiling point due to different possibilities of interaction.

Acidity/Basicity

There are several important structural properties of acids that affect their strength. The first is the number of protons, and also the addition of a functional group that can make the molecule amphoteric, which means having both acid and base properties. Some molecules, like water, are able to either donate a proton or accept a proton. As a result, they are both slightly acidic and slightly basic, depending on the surrounding conditions.

Molecules that have multiple protons are generally more acidic than those with a single proton. However, after each proton dissociates, the likelihood of the following proton dissociating will drop.

A good example of this is phosphoric acid, H_3PO_4. Phosphoric acid has three protons, but after each proton leaves, the remaining phosphate functional group becomes more negatively charged, and further reduces the likelihood of another proton leaving:

$$H_3PO_{4(s)} + H_2O_{(l)} \rightleftharpoons H_3O^+_{(aq)} + H_2PO_4^-{}_{(aq)} \qquad K_{a1} = 7.25 \times 10^{-3}$$

$$H_2PO_4^-{}_{(aq)} + H_2O_{(l)} \rightleftharpoons H_3O^+_{(aq)} + HPO_4^{2-}{}_{(aq)} \qquad K_{a2} = 6.31 \times 10^{-8}$$

$$HPO_4^{2-}{}_{(aq)} + H_2O_{(l)} \rightleftharpoons H_3O^+_{(aq)} + PO_4^{3-}{}_{(aq)} \qquad K_{a3} = 4.80 \times 10^{-13}$$

The acid dissociation constant for the first proton is relatively high, and results in a pH of around 3. However, after the second proton has dissociated, the Ka value of 4.8×10^{-13} means that at neutral pH values or slightly acidic pH, the HPO_4^{2-} molecule is actually more likely to act as a base than an acid. For this reason, phosphoric acid is considered an amphoteric molecule once the first proton has been lost.

The second important factor in acid strength is the strength of the bonds that hold the proton. This is influenced by three sub-factors:

- The strength of the actual bond

- The polarity of the bond that is caused by electronegativity differences

- The stability of the conjugate base of the acid

The stronger a bond is, the less likely it is that the proton will be able to leave. Likewise, if the bond is very polar, that means that there are both covalent and ionic forces holding the proton in place. A good example is that of hydrofluoric acid (HF). Because the fluorine molecule is so electronegative, the bond is highly polarized. The hydrogen atom has a positive charge, and the fluorine atom has a negative charge. The combination of the shared electrons and also the bond polarity means that hydrofluoric acid is a weaker acid. The following figure shows the correlation between bond strength, polarity, and acidity.

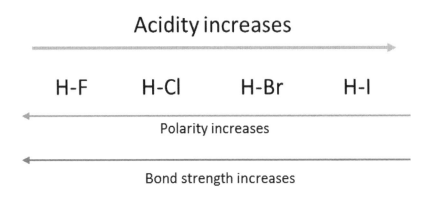

Figure 33

The last factor is the conjugate base stability. Recall that if a proton leaves a molecule, the proton is positively charged, and the conjugate base becomes negatively charged. However, chemical molecules prefer to be neutrally charged in order to maintain the highest stability. As a result, if the negative charge can be spread out over numerous atoms, the conjugate base is more stable and a proton is more likely to leave.

Hypochlorous acid, an acid with the structure HOCl, is a relatively weak acid because when the proton leaves, the resulting conjugate base OCl^- is not stable. As a result, the molecule will prefer to stay as HOCl.

On the other hand, chloric acid, $HOClO_2$, has a much more stable conjugate base, in the structure seen below:

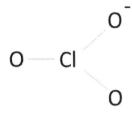

Figure 34

The negative charge can be delocalized to any of the three oxygen atoms, resulting in three possible resonance structures. Because of this delocalization of charge, the molecule is more stable and results in a strong acid.

On the AP Chemistry exam, a more difficult free response question correlating acid structure with acidity may look like this:

Question: In a carboxylic acid, shown below, the addition of a strongly electronegative functional group to the carbon indicated would likely have what effects on the molecule, if any? Explain.

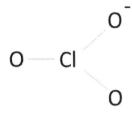

Figure 35

61

To answer, we need to consider three factors:

1. We know that carboxylic acids are weak acids. They do not dissociate completely. This indicates that adding a functional group to the acid <u>will have an effect</u>. Adding functional groups to strong acids does not usually affect their activity.

2. Second, we note that the functional group is strongly electronegative. Strongly electronegative groups will increase the polarity of the molecule.

3. Finally, we note that we have added the functional group to a carbon, but it is <u>not the carbon in the carboxyl group</u>. This means that any effect will be diminished.

Answer: The acidity of this acid (propionic acid) would be slightly decreased. This is due to the addition of a strongly electronegative group to the carbon adjacent to the carboxyl group. Strongly electronegative groups on acids will increase the polarity of the acid molecule. When the polarity of the acid molecule increases, the corresponding acidity decreases. The acidity will decrease only slightly because the functional group was added to the alpha, or adjacent carbon, to the acidic group. If the functional group had been added directly to the carboxylic acid functional group's carbon, then the effects would be more pronounced, and the likelihood of the acidic proton leaving would be further decreased.

Phase Changes

A "phase" is a description of the physical characteristics of a material. There are four phases: Solid, Liquid, Gas, and Plasma. The plasma phase occurs when a substance has been heated and pressurized past its critical point, resulting in a new phase that has liquid & gas properties.

- *Solid*: A solid is a dense phase characterized by close bonds between all molecules in the solid.

- *Liquid*: A liquid is a fluid phase characterized by loose bonds between molecules in the liquid.

- *Gas*: A gas is a very disperse phase characterized by the lack of, or very weak bonds, between molecules.

A substance will change phase depending on the temperature and pressure. As temperature increases, the phase will progress from solid to liquid to gas. As pressure increases, the opposite is true, and the phase will progress from gas to liquid to solid. In order to understand the phase change properties of a substance, we can use a phase diagram. Below is the phase diagram for water:

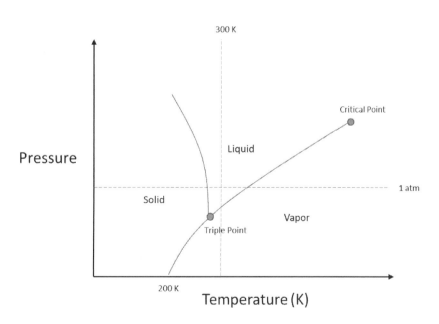

Figure 36

65

In the phase diagram there are two points that are interesting to note:

- *Triple Point*: at this point, all three phases exist: solid, liquid, and gas

- *Critical Point*: at this point, water enters the plasma phase

The phase diagram can be used to interpret what will happen to water as the temperature and pressure change. We can see that at normal pressure of 1 atm, water will transition from a solid to a liquid at around 273 K, or 0 C, which makes sense. The intersection of the two red dotted lines is room temperature and atmospheric pressure, at which water is a liquid. As we continue along the temperature spectrum, we can see that water will turn into a vapor.

One interesting property to note for water is that at room temperature, regardless of the pressure, water will never turn into a solid.

Nuclear Chemistry and Radioactivity

Radioactive decay is a phenomenon in which an unstable atom releases a particle of ionizing radiation, in the form of an alpha particle, beta particle, or gamma ray.

Alpha Particle Decay

An alpha particle is two protons and two neutrons, with a total mass of 4 amu. Due to the large size of the particle, it typically cannot penetrate skin or even paper, and is not harmful unless ingested. The majority of radioactive elements are able to produce alpha particles. When an alpha particle is produced, the atomic number of the element is also reduced, changing the element itself. For example, the emission of an alpha particle by polonium 210 will form lead-206.

Beta Particle Decay

A beta particle is a high energy high speed electron. It has very little mass and can penetrate the human skin, but is stopped by nearly all metals, no matter how thin.

Gamma Radiation

Gamma rays have no mass, unlike alpha and beta particles. They are emitted from high atomic number radioactive materials in association with the formation of alpha and beta particles. Gamma radiation can penetrate thick metal, even lead, of up to several inches thick.

Half-Life

As elements decay, they will change into a more stable form, eventually losing all their radioactive properties. The measurement of the time needed for one half of the atoms to lose their radioactivity is the half-life. A table of a sample element half-life of 20 years is shown below:

Time (yr)	20	40	60	80	100
Mass	1	0.5	0.25	0.125	0.0675

The equation for the calculation of half-life is:

$$t_{1/2} = \frac{\ln(2)}{\lambda} = \tau \ln(2)$$

Where lambda is the decay constant, and tau is the mean lifetime of a particle before decay.

On the AP Exam, the questions on nuclear chemistry may test you on the properties of each type of radiation, and also on the half-life of a particular compound. An example question is seen below:

Question: In medicine, radioactive iodine is typically used in some magnetic resonance imaging (MRI) or spectroscopic methods in order to better visualize the presence of some compounds in the patient's body. Iodine-131 has a half-life of 8 days. If the health standard is that a patient cannot have more than 0.1g of iodine-131 in their body after 30 days, what is the maximum initial loading of iodine?

Here are the steps we need to take:

1. Calculate the number of half-lives after 30 days.

    30 days/8 days = 3.75 half-lives.

2. Calculate the decay constant.

    8 days = ln(2)/lambda. Lambda = 0.0866

3. Calculate the mean lifetime:

    1/lambda = tau = 11.54 days

Answer: If 3.75 half-lives have passed, then the original amount that we can load is 0.1g x $2^{3.75}$ = 1.345 grams of the radioactive iodine.

Ideal Gas Law & Gases

A gas is defined as a collection of atoms or molecules that are loosely connected and moving about in random directions. The interactions between each atom and molecule in a gas are extremely weak, and for this reason, gases have a low density compared to liquids and solids. However, due to their increased activity, the internal energy of a molecule in the gaseous phase is higher than that of a molecule in the liquid or solid phase.

There is a difference between <u>real gases</u> and <u>ideal gases</u>. Real gases are what we experience in the real world. These gases are compressible, have intermolecular interactions, and may react. The concept of an ideal gas is an "idealized" version of a gas that simplifies calculations in chemistry. An ideal gas assumes the following rules:

- Each gas molecule occupies a very small volume (close to zero) compared to the overall volume of the container.

- All collisions between gas molecules are perfectly elastic.

- There are no attractive or repulsive forces acting on the gas molecules.

- The gas molecules are in constant motion and move completely randomly.

Based on these conditions, the ideal gas law was developed, which states that:

$$PV = nRT$$

Where P is the pressure, V is the volume, n is the number of mols of gas, R is the ideal gas constant, and T is the temperature. The ideal gas constant value can change depending on the units used. The three most common constants used are below:

Value	Units
8.314	J/(mol*K)
0.08205	(L*atm)/(mol*K)
1.987	cal/(mol*K)

When solving the ideal gas equation, you need to make sure that the ideal gas constant that you have chosen has the correct units to cancel out the remaining units. An example of an ideal gas constant problem is given below:

Question: What is the volume of 1.5 mols of gas at a temperature of 25 °C, 1 atm?

To solve:

1. The temperature units don't match, so we need to convert to Kelvin. K = C + 273. The temperature is 298 kelvin.

2. We choose the correct gas constant, which is 0.08205 (L*atm)/(mol*K), because the pressure we are given is in atmospheres.

3. We set up the equation to solve for volume, and substitute our values:

$$V = nRT/P$$

$$V = \frac{1.5 \ mols \ \times 0.08205 \ \frac{L \times atm}{mol \ \times K} \times 298 \ K}{1 \ atm}$$

At this point, we note that all the units will cancel out except for liters, which fits our solution for volume. Then, we perform the calculation, and find that...

Answer: V = 36.676 liters.

Boyle's Law

Boyle's law is a statement used to derive the ideal gas law. It states that the pressure and volume of a gas are inversely correlated. The equation for Boyle's law is stated as:

$$P1V1 = P2V2$$

Based on this, we can derive an equation that is very helpful to us:

$$P2 = \frac{P1V1}{V2} \; or \; V2 = \frac{P1V1}{P2}$$

This rule is true if the temperature and the number of mols of gas remain constant. Thus, according to this correlation, the volume of a gas is directly proportional to the pressure. This relationship is logarithmic in nature. For example, let's say that the initial volume is 1 liter and the initial pressure is 1 atm. The following table shows the change of volume with pressure:

P1	1 atm	1 atm	1 atm	1 atm	1 atm	1 atm	1 atm
P2	1.5 atm	2.0 atm	2.5 atm	3.0 atm	3.5 atm	4.0 atm	4.5 atm
V1	1 L	1 L	1 L	1 L	1 L	1 L	1 L
V2	0.66 L	0.50 L	0.4 L	0.33 L	0.285 L	0.25 L	0.22 L

If we plot this information on a graph, we obtain the following graph:

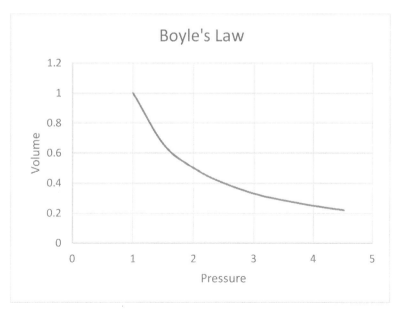

Figure 37

Charles' Law

Charles' Law, another law used to derive the ideal gas equation, states that temperature is directly correlated to volume for a gas, assuming the pressure and number of mols of gas remain constant. According to this correlation:

$$\frac{V1}{T1} = \frac{V2}{T2}$$

This means that if we rearrange the equation, the useful equations we derive are:

$$V2 = T2 \times \frac{V1}{T1} \; and \; T2 = V2 \times \frac{T1}{V1}$$

In the same manner as Boyle's law, we can use these equations to calculate a shift in volume based on temperature. However, Boyle's law's correlation is <u>linear</u>, not logarithmic. If we use values as seen in the table and graph below, the linear trend is clearly seen:

T1 (K)	273	273	273	273	273	273	273
T2 (K)	273	293	313	333	353	373	393
V1 (L)	1 L	1 L	1 L	1 L	1 L	1 L	1 L
V2 (L)	1	1.07	1.15	1.22	1.29	1.37	1.44

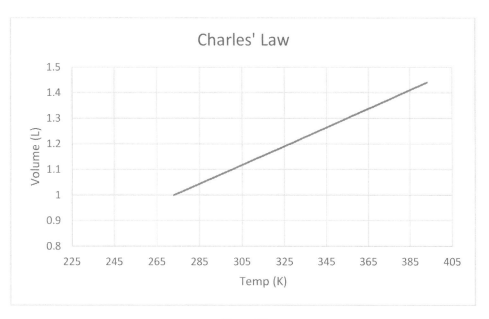

Figure 38

The conclusion that we gain from these two laws is that temperature and pressure both have effects on the volume of a gas. The temperature relationship is linear. However, the pressure relationship is logarithmic. If the pressure decreases to a very low amount, then the volume of the gas expands very quickly. If the pressure increases to a very high amount, the volume of gas will start shrinking more slowly.

Standard Temperature and Pressure

When working with gases, there is a concept called standard temperature and pressure that can be used to estimate the volume of a gas at standard conditions.

The standard temperature is 0 C, or 298 K. The standard pressure is 1 atm, or 101.35 kPA. At these two standards, 1 mol of ideal gas is known to occupy 22.4 liters.

Partial Pressures and Mixtures

What happens to the ideal gas law if we are dealing with a mixture of gas? Assuming that the mixture of gas does not react and otherwise follows the ideal gas laws, the same theories can be applied. In a mixture of gases, each individual gas contributes to the overall pressure in the same proportion as its number of mols, known as the partial pressure.

The partial pressure of a gas is thus related in the following equation:

$$P_p = X_a \times P_{total}$$

Where the partial pressure of a gas = mol fraction of the gas multiplied by the total pressure. For example, oxygen makes up about 21% of the atmosphere. If the total pressure of the atmosphere is 1 atm, we can state that oxygen's partial pressure is 0.21 atm, according to the partial pressure equation.

Gas Diffusion

Diffusion of gases is similar to the diffusion of solutes inside a solution. In gases, a concentration gradient will form, and gases will diffuse from high concentrations to low concentrations.

Real Gases and Gas Reactions

Real gases and gas mixtures that react <u>do not follow the ideal gas law</u>. Due to their interaction, their actual volume and pressure may be greater than or less than predicted by the ideal gas law. Especially in mixtures of gases that react, such as a mixture of N_2O_4 and NO_2, which interchange between each other, the volume of the gas is unpredictable and depends on the temperature and pressure, which increases or decreases the reaction rate. If a problem states that the gas reacts or has intermolecular interactions, the ideal gas law cannot be used.

Major differences between real gases and ideal gases:

- At high pressures, real gases will differ in behavior from ideal gases. For example, although the ideal gas law may predict the same volume at 1 atmosphere of pressure, if the pressure is increased to 20 atm, the ideal gas law will no longer be valid, and will produce a result that is not correct.

- At high temperatures, real gases will differ in behavior from ideal gases. A good example of a real gas in this scenario is steam. At high temperatures, water vapor has strong intermolecular hydrogen bonding forces that result in a smaller volume than predicted by the ideal gas law.

On the AP Exam, questions involving gases will usually ask you to solve for a missing variable using the idea gas equation, or identify an ideal gas or real gas. Questions will sometimes combine stoichiometry and the ideal gas question.

Question: 45 liters of carbon dioxide is reacted with an excess of hydrogen to form methanol and water. This is a high temperature reaction that takes place at 1000 K and 1 atm. What is the volume of methanol vapor formed? Assume all gases act ideally.

In the first step, we need to assess all the information in this problem.

- We are given a volume of gas

- We are given the names of all the reactants

- We are given a pressure and temperature

Using this information, we see that we can solve for the number of mols of carbon dioxide, so we need to write a chemical reaction equation. The basic equation is:

$$CO_2 + H_2 \rightarrow CH_3OH + H_2O$$

After balancing, we find that:

$$CO_2 + 3\ H_2 \rightarrow CH_3OH + H_2O$$

We use the ideal gas law to find the number of mols of carbon dioxide. Because we are given pressure in atm, we will use the constant 0.08206 L*atm/mol*K.

We need to set up and solve the equation for "n":

$$PV = nRT$$

$$n = \frac{PV}{RT}$$

$$n = \frac{1\ atm \times 45\ L}{0.08206\ \frac{L \times atm}{mol \times K} \times 1000\ K}$$

$$n = 0.548\ mols, round\ to\ 0.55$$

So now we know that 0.55 mols of carbon dioxide are present in the reaction. Now, we solve for the amount of product in mols, then use the ideal gas law to calculate the volume. The stoichiometric ratio of methanol to carbon dioxide is 1:1. Thus, if we use 0.55 mols of carbon dioxide, 0.55 mols of methanol are formed. Because the temperature, pressure, and "n" remain the same, we don't have to solve the ideal gas equation again!

Answer: The volume of methanol will be 45 liters.

Solubility

Solubility is defined as the ability of a solute to dissolve into a solvent. A classic example of this is salt (NaCl) dissolving into water. The opposite reaction of solvation is precipitation, in which a compound comes out of the solution and forms a liquid.

When a solution has reached the maximum amount of solute, it is called a saturated solution. For salt, the saturation concentration at room temperature is 36.09 grams per 100 grams of water, or a solution of 36%. At this point, any further salt added to the water will not dissolve and will remain as a solid. The solubility equilibrium constant can be determined experimentally, and follows this basic form:

$$K_{sp} = [A]^n [B]^x$$

Where A and B are dissolved ions, and n and x are their stoichiometric ratios. For example, the stoichiometric ratios for an $MgCl_2$ are 1 for Mg and 2 for Cl, respectively.

Factors Affecting Solubility and Its Rules

There are many factors that can affect the solubility of a compound. One effect is called the common ion effect, where two compounds share a common ion. When the two compounds are mixed into a solvent, the presence of the common ion reduces the solubility of each compound.

For example, if we mix NaCl and $MgCl_2$, they share the common ion of chlorine. As a result, the maximum saturation of chlorine ion in water will be reached between the saturation of either sodium or magnesium is reached. This causes a reduction in the overall solubility. Instead of a solution of 36% NaCl, we may only be able to dissolve 20% NaCl in water.

Important Rules

You'll need to know these for the test!

- Almost all ionic compounds that contain nitrate (NO_2^{2-}), and ammonium (NH_4^+) are soluble.

- All ionic compounds with Cl, Br, and I are soluble, except for silver, mercury, and lead.

- All compounds with sulfate (SO_4^{2-}) are soluble, except for silver, mercury, and lead.

These will probably be provided in the examination, but you should know them, too:

- Heavier alkaline metals are soluble when paired with sulfides or hydroxides

- These compounds are insoluble, unless mentioned above: carbonates (CO_3^{2-}), phosphates (PO_4), and hydroxides (OH^-). For example, iron hydroxide is insoluble.

Reactions

Introduction to Chemical Reactions

There are two types of reactions: physical and chemical. A physical reaction does not result in a change in the chemical composition of a reactant, but only the physical structure. For example, a change of state, or a crystallization reaction, is a physical reaction.

A chemical reaction is one in which the molecular structure or composition of the compound has been changed. Some basic chemical reactions include replacement, synthesis, decomposition, and combustion reactions.

In a chemical reaction, there is a conservation of mass. The inputs, or reactant mass, must equal the outputs, or products. Whenever you see a chemical reaction equation, make sure that the inputs equal the outputs. This is called balancing the reaction.

Important Chemical Reaction Terms

Stoichiometric Coefficient

The stoichiometric coefficient is the ratio of a chemical in a reaction to other reactants. In the reaction equation below, the stoichiometric coefficient of oxygen is 2.

$$CH_4 + 2\ O_2 \rightarrow CO_2 + 2\ H_2O$$

Reaction Completion

If a reaction goes "to completion", this means all of the reactants have been used.

Limiting Reagent

If there is a reagent which limits the use of another reagent, then it is the limiting reagent.

Yield

The yield of a reaction is the actual yield divided by the theoretical yield.

Basic Types of Reactions

There are five basic types of reactions that you should be able to recognize without any aids or hints.

Synthesis

In a synthesis reaction, two or more reactants will form a single product.

$$A + B \rightarrow C$$

Decomposition

In a decomposition reaction, a single reactant will decompose into two products Decomposition reactions typically require an input of energy.

$$A \rightarrow B + C$$

Single Displacement

In a single displacement reaction, one reactant will dissociate, and its complement ion will react with another species in solution.

$$AB + C \rightarrow A + BC$$

Double Displacement

In a double displacement reaction, two reactants will dissociate, and interchange complement ions.

$$AB + CD \rightarrow AC + BD$$

Combustion

In a combustion reaction, a fuel (alkane or carbohydrate are typical) will be oxidized by oxygen to form carbon dioxide and water.

$$C_xH_yO_z + O_2 \rightarrow CO_2 + H_2O$$

Synthesis/Combination Reactions

A synthesis reaction will usually involve the combination of two separate species to form a third, new compound. One of the reactions in this group is the formation of an ionic compound by the combination of a metal and a non-metal element.

Most metals are not very electronegative, and will react readily with non-metals such as nitrogen or oxygen, which have higher electronegativity values. A standard reaction series with group 1 metals follows this formula:

$$2M_s + X_2 \rightarrow 2(MX)$$

For this reaction, the metal (M) is a group 1 metal, such as lithium or sodium in solid form. X is a halogen non-metal. It can then react with the non-metal, usually in gaseous form, to create a product that has one of each atom. An example reaction involving potassium is:

$$2K + Cl_2 \rightarrow 2KCl$$

Similarly, other metals can react in this fashion with non-metals to form ionic compounds. The ratios will not always be same, but the general principle of the reaction is maintained. In this synthesis reaction, a metal will react with a non-metal to form a new ionic compound.

Compound Synthesis Reactions

In a second type of synthesis reaction, two compounds, and not individual elements, will react to form a third, new compound. A requirement of this reaction is that the reactants are compounds, such as CaO or MgO. In addition, only a single product is formed, as a result of the combination of the two or more reactants. An example is shown below:

$$SO_3 + H_2SO_4 \rightarrow H_2S_2O_7$$

An important note about synthesis reactions - both those involving simple elements and compounds - is that these reactions are irreversible. Once the reaction has occurred, the corresponding backwards reaction will not happen. Technically speaking, the reverse reaction could happen, but would require a very high input of energy and perhaps a catalyst.

Acid Base Reactions and pH

Definitions

There are three definitions of acids or bases: the Arrhenius, Bronsted-Lowry, and Lewis acid definitions. For the majority of chemical reactions in the scope of the exam, the Bronsted-Lowry definition of an acid will be used.

Arrhenius

An acid is a substance that produces H+ hydrogen ions in aqueous solution. A base is a substance that produces hydroxide ions OH- in aqueous solution.

Bronsted-Lowry

An acid is anything that donates a proton H+, and a base is anything that accepts a proton.

Lewis

An acid is anything is able to accept a pair of electrons, and a base is anything that can donate a pair of electrons.

What is pH?

The pH of a solution is a measure of the acidity or basicity of the solution. A low pH is acidic, and a high pH is basic. The pH scale runs from 0 to 14. A pH of 7 is that of water with no dissolved ions, and is considered neutral. pH can be calculated by:

$$pH = -\log(H+)$$

Where H+ is the hydrogen ion concentration of the solution. In the determination of pH in a solution, the most important factor is the dissociation constant, or K_a of the acid or base. A strong acid or base has a K_a value that goes to infinity.

For this reason, the concept of pKa, which is the log scale of Ka, was developed:

$$pKa = -\log(Ka)$$

From this scale, we can understand that an acid with a pKa of less than -2 (which has a corresponding Ka of 100 or greater) is a strong acid. Strong acids will dissociate at a rate of 99% or greater in aqueous solution.

Any other acid is considered a weak acid, and may have pKa values between -2 and 50. Weak acid dissociate at rates of 98% to less than 1%.

Examples of strong acids:

- Hydrobromic acid (HBr)
- Hydrochloric acid (HCl)
- Sulfuric acid (H_2SO_4)

Examples of weak acids:

- Acetic Acid ($C_2H_4O_2$)
- Formic acid (HCOOH)
- Butryic acid ($C_4H_8O_2$)

Weak Acid pH

The pH of a strong acid is easy to determine: we simply calculate the molarity of strong acid, assuming it dissociates completely, and input the value of the hydrogen ion molarity into the pH equation.

Determining the pH of a weak acid is more complex. This is because we must first determine how much acid has been dissociated, and then calculate the pH. The following is an example problem:

A student has placed 10g of acetic acid into a 1 liter solution of water. The pKa of acetic acid is 4.75. What is the resulting pH of the solution?

1. First, the molarity of the solution is calculated. Acetic acid has a molar mass of 60g/mol. Thus, the solution is 0.166 molar.

2. Next, we find the dissociation constant. pKa = -log (Ka). Thus, Ka = 10^{-pKa}. We find that the dissociation constant is 1.78 x 10^{-5}.

3. Now, we can set up the acid dissociation equation:

$$Ka = \frac{[H^+][A^-]}{[HA]}$$

4. The original concentration is known: 0.166 molar. Acetic acid is a monoprotic acid, as it can only donate one proton. Thus, we reformulate the equation to be:

$$1.78 \times 10^{-5} = \frac{[x][x]}{[0.166 - x]}$$

5. We can now solve for x using algebra. This can be quite challenging! However, it can be simplified by an assumption. If we assume that x is very small compared to 0.166, we can remove it from the denominator. This simplifies the problem, and we find that x = 0.001718. This is the concentration of hydrogen ions in the solution.

6. Using the pH equation, we set it up to be pH = -log(0.001718), and find that the pH is 2.76.

There are several important facts that are sometimes incorrectly applied. The pKa is not equivalent to the pH. It is a measure of the tendency of a weak acid to dissociate. The pKa will change with temperature and solvent. Most measured pKa values are for dissociation into water at room temperature.

Next, we have to remember to set up the dissociation equation properly. If it is a diprotic acid, then the equation becomes more complex. There is a different dissociation constant for each proton in an acid.

Acid-Base Reactions & Titrations

Acids and bases, by their nature, eliminate each other when placed into an aqueous solution to form water. As a result, if an equal amount of strong acid is mixed with an equal amount of strong base, the pH will remain at 7. The two will interact and neutralize one another.

This concept of neutralization forms the basis for pH titrations. A pH titration is used to determine the pKa of a weak acid or weak base. During the titration, a weak acid is titrated by a strong base until two points are determined: the half equivalence point, and the equivalence point, shown in the diagram below.

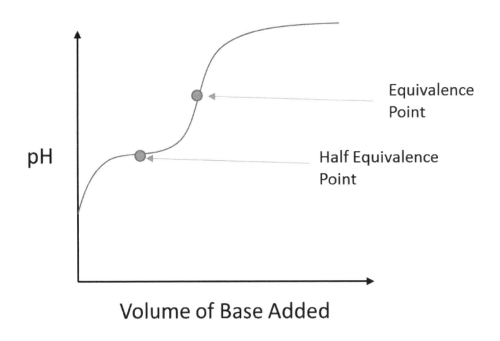

Figure 39

- At the equivalence point, all of the acid is dissociated, and has been completely neutralized by the base.

- At the half equivalence point, exactly half of the acid has been dissociated, such that A- = HA. At this point, the pKa = the pH.

You can learn more about titration setup in the Laboratory section of this guide.

Oxidation Reduction Reactions

An oxidation or reduction reaction is one in which there is an exchange of electrons. The species that loses electrons is oxidized, and the species that gains electrons is reduced. A simple mnemonic to remember this is OIL RIG.

- **O**xidation
- **I**nvolves
- **L**oss
- **R**eduction
- **I**nvolves
- **G**ain

Oxidation State

The assessment of the oxidation state of an atom is important for understanding redox reactions. The oxidation state is the current number of electrons an atom has, and the charge associated. Many elements in their natural state tend to be oxidized. For example, oxygen naturally has an oxidation state of -2, possessing two additional electrons. Iron naturally has an oxidation state of +2 or +3, having lost 2 or three electrons to other species.

In general, the following rules can help provide guidelines for determining oxidation state. Note that there are exceptions to this table, especially for sulfur and phosphorus:

Group 1 Elements (Alkali metals, Na, Li, etc.)	+1
Group 2 Elements (Alkaline earth, Be, Mg, etc.)	+2
Group 15 Elements (N, P, etc.)	-3
Group 16 Elements (O, S, etc.)	-2
Group 17 Elements (Halogens, F, Cl, etc.)	-1

Below is a sample reaction:

$$CuSO_4 + 2NaOH \rightarrow Cu(OH)_2 + Na_2SO_4$$

We now must determine the oxidation states of each reactant:

$Cu = 2+$

$SO4 = 2-$

From this, we can determine that if each O is -2, the sulfur must be +6.

$Na = +1$

$OH = -1$

From this, we know that the oxygen is -2 and the hydrogen is +1, for a total of -1.

Then, we look at the products:

$Cu = 2+$

$OH = -1$

$Na = +1$

$SO4 = 2-$

Is this a redox reaction? The answer is no! The oxidation state of the species participating in this reaction has not changed. By comparing the oxidation states before and after the reaction, we reach the conclusion that this is a double substitution reaction, with no change in oxidation state. Here is an example of a redox reaction:

$$2\ Mg(s) + O_2(g) \longrightarrow 2\ MgO(s)$$

In this reaction, we see that Mg starts off with no charge, or an oxidation state of 0. Oxygen also starts off with no charge, being covalently bonded to another oxygen. After the reaction, which involves the oxidation of magnesium, the magnesium is now +2 in charge and the O is -2 in charge. Magnesium has been oxidized and oxygen has been reduced. The resulting compound is now an ionic compound.

This brings to light another fact. By the very nature of oxidation reductions, the product formed must possess ionic bonds. If the product only has covalent bonds, in which electrons are shared and not gained or lost, then it cannot be a redox reaction.

Question: A student wants to perform the following reaction:

$$KMnO_4\ (aq) + H_2S\ (aq) + H_2SO_4\ (aq) \rightarrow K_2SO_4\ (aq) + MnSO_4\ (aq) + S\ (s)$$

If 1.5 mols of potassium permanganate are used in the solution, how many mols of electrons are produced or consumed on the reactant side of the equation? Which species is being oxidized and which species is being reduced?

After we finish balancing the equation, we get:

$$2\ KMnO_4 + 5\ H_2S + 3\ H_2SO_4 \rightarrow 1\ K_2SO_4 + 2\ MnSO_4 + 5\ S + 8\ H_2O$$

In this problem, we need to add water to the products side of the equation in order to balance all the hydrogens and oxygen that are produced. This is an appropriate addition because we are working in an <u>aqueous solution</u> that is able to absorb extra protons generated from the reaction. However, as a result, the oxygen balance will be slightly off.

Next, we need to find oxidation states for the products and the reactants.

- **$KMnO_4$:** K +1, O -2, Mn +7 – The oxygen has a -2 charge and the potassium has a +1 charge. Since the molecule is neutral, this means that Mn must have a +7 charge.

- **H_2S:** H +1, S -2

- **H_2SO_4:** H +1, O -2, S +6

Products side:

- **K_2SO_4: K +1, S +6, O -2:** there is no change in oxidation state here

- **$MnSO_4$: Mn +2, S +6, O -2:** the manganese ion has gained electrons

- **S: S 0:** the sulfur atom has no charge, and thus has lost electrons

From this analysis, we concluded that the manganese is gaining electrons, and is becoming reduced in this reaction. The sulfur is losing electrons and is becoming oxidized. According to stoichiometry, we need to produce 10 electrons on the left hand side in order to convert Mn 7+ to Mn 2+ (there are two Mn atoms). This means that sulfur needs to lose 10 electrons. We have five molecules of H_2S, and thus five sulfur atoms. This check ensures that we are both producing and consuming enough electrons.

Answer: Manganese is being reduced and is gaining five electrons. Sulfur is being oxidized and losing two electrons. On the reactant side of the equation, 10 mols of electrons are produced and consumed.

This problem is significantly more difficult than the problems you will encounter on the AP exam. However, if you can do this problem, the test will be easy!

Redox Titrations

A redox titration is used to determine the concentration of reducible or oxidizable materials in a solution. For example, if you have a solution that has some iron, chromium, or copper in it, you can perform a redox titration in order to determine the full concentration.

The most common chemical used in redox titrations is potassium permanganate, $KMnO_4$. It is a very strong oxidizing agent, and has the benefit of having a bright pink/magenta color. The potassium permanganate is added slowly to the solution until the color disappears, at which point the titration is complete. The quantity of potassium permanganate solution tells us the amount of oxidizable material that was in the solution.

Reaction Potentials and the Galvanic Cell

In a redox reaction, electrons must be transferred. Through the movement of the electrons during the course of the reaction, electric potential is generated. The generation of the electric potential in this type of reaction is also the basis for the chemical battery. The larger the potential generated, the better the battery.

In a galvanic cell, two chemical compounds are placed on opposite sides of a cell. One side of the cell is the anode, which generates electrons by oxidizing the anode material. The other side of the cell is the cathode, which receives the electrons by reducing the cathode material. The flow of electrons between the two cells generates the current used in the battery. The difference in potential between the half reactions present in the anode and cathode create the voltage, or driving force.

Below is an example of a galvanic cell half reaction set:

$$Zn(s) \rightarrow Zn^{2+} + 2e^-\text{ Oxidation, Anode}$$

$$Cu^{2+} + 2e^- \rightarrow Cu(s)\text{ Reduction, Cathode}$$

On the exam, you need to be able to identify the anode and cathode of a galvanic cell by determining which material is being oxidized or reduced.

Question: Given the following table of standard reduction potentials, design a galvanic cell that will produce the most voltage. Write the overall equation for this reaction, and indicate which species is being reduced. Identify which material will be on the cathode and which will be on the anode.

	Reactant 1		Reactant 2	Potential
1	$Ba(OH)_2 + 2e^-$	←→	$Ba + 2\,OH^-$	−2.99
2	$Ca2+ + 2\,e-$	←→	$Ca(s)$	−2.868
3	$Mg2+ + 2\,e-$	←→	$Mg(s)$	−2.372
4	$Cr3+ + 3\,e-$	←→	$Cr(s)$	−0.74
5	$Pt2+ + 2\,e-$	←→	$Pt(s)$	+1.188
6	$MnO_4- + 4\,H^+ + 3\,e-$	←→	$MnO_2(s) + 2\,H_2O$	+1.70

First, we want to choose the best half reactions. The half reactions that will produce the most voltage will have the greatest potential difference. In this case, it is reaction 1 with reaction 6. This nets us a potential difference of 4.7! The reaction will then be:

$$Ba(OH)_2 + 2e^- + MnO_2 + 2H_2O \leftrightarrow Ba + 2OH^- + MnO_4^- + 4H^+ + 3e-$$

Unfortunately, this equation is not balanced in terms of electrons, so we need to produce the same number of electrons on both sides of the equation. The easiest way to do this is to multiple the barium half reaction by 3 and the manganese half reaction by 2.

$$3\ Ba(OH)_2 + 6e^- + 2MnO_2 + 4H_2O \longleftrightarrow 3\ Ba + 6\ OH^- + 2\ MnO_4^- + 8H^+ + 6e-$$

Now, there are equal amounts of electrons on both sides, and the rest of the equation is balanced as well! We can proceed to designing the galvanic cell.

In the reactants side, the barium atom has a +2 charge and the Mn has a +2 charge. On the products side, the Barium has a +0 charge and the Mn has a +9 charge. This means that the barium is gaining electrons and being reduced and the manganese is losing electrons and being oxidized. Remember:

- Cathode = reduction
- Anode = oxidation

Thus, the cathode material should be barium, and the anode material should be manganese oxide.

Reaction Stoichiometry

Stoichiometry is the relationship of the relative quantities of the reactants and products in a chemical reaction. Having a correct stoichiometry is vital to solving pretty much any chemistry problem correctly. The basic principle behind stoichiometry is the conservation of mass. Whatever enters a system must also exit the system. As a result, a chemical equation as seen below is not correct:

$$C_3H_8 + O_2 \longrightarrow H_2O + CO_2$$

In this example, there are three carbons entering the reaction on the reactants side, but only one carbon leaving on the products side. This cannot be correct! In order to make the equation correct, we have to go through the process of balancing the equation, resulting in the following reaction:

$$C_3H_8 + 5O_2 \longrightarrow 4H_2O + 3CO_2$$

The steps to balance a chemical equation are:

1. Check the reactants side and understand the reaction coefficients on that side.
2. Pick an element to work with. In the example above, we would pick carbon.
3. Change the stoichiometric coefficients on the products side as necessary to make the element balanced. In the example above, we would add a coefficient of 3 to the CO_2 product.
4. Check the equation for imbalances. In the example above, now that we have added 3 CO_2, the oxygen is now unbalanced.
5. Repeat the process for the unbalanced terms.

Often, a problem may not give you a clean equation to work with. Instead, they will tell you the mass of reactants in a problem, and you will need to convert the mass into mols. If that is the case, use the formula on the next page:

$$\#mols = \frac{mass}{formula\ weight}$$

Here, we will perform a relatively difficult stoichiometry problem to give a good example of the steps required.

Question: A scientist wants to react 71.5 grams of iron oxide with chlorine in order to form the product iron (II) chloride and oxygen gas. Find the correct stoichiometric equation for this reaction and predict the mass in grams of iron chloride that will form.

Wow! This is quite a complicated problem! We're not given an equation to start with, the amount of reactants is given in grams and not mols, and not only do we have to find the correct equation, but we also need to predict the mass of the product formed! Where do we start?

The first thing we need to do is find out how many mols of iron oxide is reacting, and also what type of iron is reacting. In the problem, it is stated that the product is iron (II) chloride, which tells us the iron has an oxidation state of +2. This doesn't look like an oxidation reduction reaction, so the oxidation state of this iron should not change. If the iron has a +2 charge, then the formula should be FeO, which has a formula weight of 71.5 grams. Great! That means we have exactly 1 mol of iron oxide.

Based on the formula of the iron oxide, we can propose the following equation:

$$FeO + Cl_2 \rightarrow FeCl_2 + O_2$$

The product is $FeCl_2$ because we are working with Fe 2+ and chlorine has a -1 charge. Now, upon examining this equation, we find that it is not balanced. The oxygen ratios are not correct. There is one oxygen atom on the reactants side and 2 on the products side. Thus, we need to make the equation:

$$2FeO + Cl_2 \rightarrow FeCl_2 + O_2$$

This fixes the balance for our oxygen, but now the iron isn't balanced. There are two iron atoms on the left side and only one on the right. We balance the iron by added a coefficient of 2 to the $FeCl_2$. This gets us to:

$$2FeO + Cl_2 \rightarrow 2FeCl_2 + O_2$$

But now the chlorine isn't balanced! There are two chlorine atoms on the left side of the equation, but four chlorine atoms on the right. So we adjust the equation one last time:

$$2FeO + 2Cl_2 \rightarrow 2FeCl_2 + O_2$$

On the left hand reactant side, we have 2 Fe, 2 O, and 4 Cl. On the right hand side we have 2 Fe, 2 O, and 4 Cl. Now that we have a balanced equation, we can find out how much iron chloride is formed.

The stoichiometric ratio is 1:1. 2 FeO's go in, and 2 $FeCl_2$ come out. That means that since we are putting in 1 mol of FeO, we should also get 1 mol of $FeCl_2$. The molar mass of $FeCl_2$ is 126.75g/mol.

Answer: We will form 126.75 grams of iron (II) chloride.

Solving stoichiometry problems will not always be this involved, but they will almost always follow the same basic steps:

1. Understand the molecular formulas of the reactants and products

2. Balance the chemical reaction equation

3. Plug in the values for mols of your reactant and determine the product

Limiting Reactant and Excess Reactant Stoichiometry

When we have an unbalanced amount (not an unbalanced equation, but amount) of a reactant in a chemical reaction, what happens? The result is usually that all of the reactant is used up, and once the reactant has been consumed, the reaction halts. As a result, the reactant that we have too little of is called a <u>limiting reagent or reactant</u>. The reactant that we have too much of is called the <u>excess reagent or reactant</u>.

The principle of limiting reagents and reactants is that we want to understand a chemical reaction and optimize it so that all of the reagents are used. If we have too little of one reagent, then the rest of the reagents won't be used. In practical applications, such as industrial manufacturing, this is costly and time consuming. Excess reactants need to be removed from your product, and the separation is not cheap!

The best way to find which reactant is the limiting reagent is to balance a stoichiometric equation and then compare the number of mols of each reactant in the equation to the amount that is existent in the stoichiometry. Follow these steps:

1. Find a balanced chemical equation for the reaction in question

2. Convert any given information in the problem into mols.

3. Calculate the mol ratio of formed products.

4. Compare the required mol ratios of reactants and products in the balanced equation to the information given in the problem.

5. Find the limiting reagent and excess reagent, and calculate the amount of excess.

Question: In animals, the process of aerobic respiration takes sugar, such as glucose, and consumes it to form carbon dioxide and water in an oxidation reaction. A reaction involving glucose is:

$$C_6H_{12}O_6 + O_2 \rightarrow CO_2 + H_2O$$

An experiment determined that the amount of glucose in the bloodstream of a cow is approximately 1.2 kg. If the cow takes in 60g of oxygen over the course of 1 hour, what is the limiting reagent, and how many mols of carbon dioxide will be formed after 1 hour? Assume that no sugar is added to the cow's bloodstream (i.e. the blood sugar level will decrease over time).

That's a pretty tough problem, and it can be hard to even think about where to start.

If we look at the rules above, we know that the first thing to do is balance the equation. We won't go over the steps again here (they're in the previous section) but after balancing, we get the following:

$$C_6H_{12}O_6 + 6\ O_2 \rightarrow 6\ CO_2 + 6\ H_2O$$

We check the atoms on the left and right side, and they match up, so all is well! We are given two values in the problem. We have 1.2 kg of glucose, and we have 60g of oxygen. Glucose has a molecular weight of 180g/mol. Thus,

$$\frac{1200g}{180g/mol} = 6.66\ mols$$

Oxygen is a diatomic gas, and has a molecular weight of 32. Thus, we have:

$$\frac{60g}{32g/mol} = 1.875\ mols$$

Great, so we have 6.666 mols of glucose, and 1.875 mols of oxygen. What next?

Looking at our balanced equation we see that the mol ratio of oxygen to glucose is 6:1. This means that if we want to react 1 mol of glucose, we need 6 mols of oxygen. Likewise, looking on the products end, the mol ratio of CO_2 to H_2O to glucose is 6:6:1.

Now that we know the ratio is 6:1, what conclusion can we draw? We have 6.66 mols of glucose. This means that we need 39.96 mols of oxygen in order to fully consume all the glucose. As we can see, we only 1.875 mols of oxygen. This means that the oxygen is the limiting reagent. We can calculate how much excess glucose there is: 1.875 mols of oxygen will react with 1.875/6 mols, or 0.313 mols of glucose.

Answer: At the end of one hour, we will have 6.34 mols of glucose and no oxygen left.

Le Chatelier's Principle

Le Chatelier's principle is the idea that a chemical system will respond to a stress by reducing that stress as much as possible. There are three major stresses that can occur in a chemical system:

1. Addition or removal of a reactant or product. If a system is already in equilibrium, addition of further reactants or products will shift the equilibrium.

2. Changing the pressure of the system. If a system, usually a gaseous one, experiences an increase or decrease of pressure, the equilibrium will change.

3. Changing the temperature of the system.

Response to Stress

When a system is stressed, it will respond to the stress by changing in some manner. This change is usually in the concentration of reactants or products. In response to each of the three stresses listed above, the following will occur:

1. If a product is added to a system in equilibrium, the equilibrium will shift to the left, and more reactants will be formed. The opposite will happen if a reactant is added to the system.

2. If the pressure is increased in the system, the reaction will shift to the right, and more products will be formed. The opposite will happen if the pressure decreases.

3. If the temperature is increased in a system, the reaction rate will increase and the reaction will shift to the right. The opposite may or may not happen if the temperature decreases.

Sample Situations involving Le Chatelier's Principle

Understanding Le Chatelier's Principle is one of the core concepts on the AP Chemistry exam, so we'll cover several example situations in which it can be applied.

Heat-Based Reaction Change

In this scenario, a problem will state a reaction type as well as provide accompanying information about the heat of reaction and give the reaction stoichiometry. An example:

A student is working on the decomposition of sulfur trioxide, a precursor to acid rain, into a less harmful sulfur dioxide. The reaction progresses as:

$$2SO_3 \,(g) \leftrightarrow 2\,SO_2\,(g) + O_2\,(g)\ \Delta H^o = 197.78\ kJ$$

She finds that the reaction is very slow at room temperature. Using Le Chatelier's Principle, how can she increase the reaction rate? In this problem, we have to use our understanding of reaction heat in order to apply Le Chatelier's Principle.

The ΔH^o value is positive. This means that energy must be put into the reaction for it to occur. The ending products of sulfur dioxide and oxygen gas have a higher energy content than the reactants. This tells us that we need to apply heat to the reaction for it to occur faster. At room temperature, the equilibrium state results in no products formed. At higher temperatures, we can shift the equilibrium to the right, increasing the product formation.

In this reaction, the increase of pressure or concentration of reactants could also have some effect. However, the dominant effect would be from temperature. This is indicated by the relatively high value of ΔH. If ΔH were lower, for example 20 kJ instead of 197 kJ, then we could reasonably state that increasing the pressure of the reaction system would also speed the reaction along.

Identifying the Thermodynamic Properties of Reactions

In this scenario, a problem will be stated in which a stress is applied to the system. You will need to be able to predict the shift in equilibrium due to the stress, and if given the shift, you need to be able to predict the thermodynamic properties of the reaction.

Example #1: A student is performing the following experiment in class:

$$2NO_2 \leftrightarrow N_2O_4 \,,\ \Delta H^o = \text{-}57.15\ kJ$$

The student increases the pressure by 2 atm. Which direction will the equilibrium of this reaction shift?

We look at the reaction and see that it is essentially a synthesis reaction. Two molecules of nitrous dioxide are becoming N_2O_4. This means that on the products side of the reaction, there is <u>half the number of mols</u> of gas as there are on the reactants side. According to Le Chatelier's principle, if a stress is introduced into a chemical system, then the system will do its best to relieve that pressure. In this case, because the pressure has been significantly raised, the reaction will shift to the right, to the products side. This is because if more products are formed, there will be fewer mols of gas in the reaction system, and according to the ideal gas law, that equates to a lower pressure.

Here is another example: A student is performing a reaction, and notes that as he increases the temperature, the reaction rate slows down. What type of reaction is this?

In this case, the key statement is that an increase of temperature is slowing down the reaction rate. This is indicative of an exothermic reaction. Exothermic reactions produce heat. However, according to the laws of thermodynamics, you cannot add low temperature heat to a high temperature system (there is more on this a little ater in the guide.)

According to Le Chatelier's principle, increasing the temperature of an exothermic reaction will actually slow the reaction down. The system will strive to maintain a lower temperature, and in order to do that, the reaction cannot progress.

The Takeaway

There are many more types of questions that can be based on Le Chatelier's principle, but these are some of the more difficult examples. When reading a question, jot down the important information:

1. Are there more mols of reactants than products, or vice versa?
2. Is a heat of reaction (ΔH) given?
3. Is a stress being introduced into the reaction system? If so, what?

Asking yourself these three questions will help you understand the direction the reaction is likely headed, and will aid you in the application of Le Chatelier's principle.

Reaction Equilibrium

Chemical equilibrium is a state reached in reversible reactions in which the rate of forward reaction equals the rate of reverse reaction. Once equilibrium has been reached, it will appear as though the reaction has stopped because there is no noticeable change in the creation of products. However, this isn't true. This is important, so be sure you understand this: <u>At chemical equilibrium, reactions are still occurring. The reaction has not stopped.</u> At equilibrium, the rates of the forward and backward reactions are equal:

$$A + B \rightarrow C + D$$

$$k[A][B] = k[C][D]$$

Initial-Change-Equilibrium (ICE)

The ICE chart is the most important tool in the assessment of equilibrium concentrations. Using the chart, we first determine the initial concentrations, followed by the change over the course of the reaction, and then we can calculate the equilibrium concentration.

$$\text{Reaction: } 2\ NH_3(g) \leftrightarrows N_2(g) + 3\ H_2(g) \quad K_c = 0.0076\ @\ 900\ K$$

The reaction above takes place in a five-liter container with three mols of ammonia gas, two mols of nitrogen and five moles of hydrogen at 900K. The K_c (equilibrium constant) is 0.0076 at that temperature. First, we calculate the molar concentration of each reactant, and place that in the first row of the table.

	NH3	N2	H2
Initial	0.6 M	0.4 M	1 M

Now, we set up the reaction equation to find our Qc, or the reaction quotient:

$$Qc = [N2][H2]^3/[NH3]^2 = [0.4][1]^3/[0.6]^2 = 1.111$$

Since Qc is larger than Kc, the reaction will progress to the left.

Qc Rules

- If Qc is greater than Kc, the reaction will progress to the left.
- If Qc is less than Kc, the reaction will proceed to the right.
- If Qc = Kc, then the reaction is at equilibrium.

Now that we know this, we can fill in the appropriate "change" in the ICE box:

	NH3	N2	H2
Initial	0.6 M	0.4 M	1 M
Change	0.6 M + 2x	0.4 M -x	1 M – 3x

Then, we can set up the equation to solve for X, and find our equilibrium concentrations:

$$Kc = 0.0076 = \frac{(0.4 - x)(1 - 3x)}{(0.6 + 2x)}$$

Problems on the AP exam will only go this far. Solving for x is beyond the scope of the AP Chemistry exam. The most important concepts that will be tested will be determination of the direction of a reaction and setting up the equation to determine the equilibrium concentrations.

If you do wish to solve the x, the simplest way is to use a guess and check method. If we see that Q_c is much greater than K_c, then we guess a large value for x to start with. If we see that Q_c is close to K_c, then we guess a smaller value of x to start with.

Chemical Kinetics

Chemical kinetics is the study of reaction mechanisms between reactants and their relationship to the rate of reaction. The math behind calculating chemical reaction rates based on kinetic data is advanced and will not be tested on the AP Exam. However, there are several important concepts (as well as their applications to simple chemical reactions) that you need to know.

Collision Theory

Collision theory refers to the idea that a chemical reaction cannot occur until two molecules which may react collide with one another.

This brings to light an important concept based on phases: In a solid, although molecules are all touching one another, there is not much movement. As a result, chemical reactions in solid phase have a low reaction rate, or none at all. A solid usually only reacts when its surface comes into contact with a liquid or gas.

In liquids or gases, molecules are able to move freely, which allows greater interaction and an increased chance that two capable molecules will react. For this reason, the majority of chemical reactions occur in the liquid phase or the gas phase. However, even if two molecules collide that could react, most of the time they do not. Take, for example, the reaction below:

$$C_6H_{12}O_6 + 6O_2 \rightarrow 6CO_2 + 6H_2O$$

This reaction is the combustion of cellulose (wood sugar) with oxygen to form carbon dioxide and water. It is a typical reaction that occurs when we burn wood in a fireplace. However, wood exists everywhere in our environment: in the forest, in our tables, in our houses. Obviously, oxygen is always in the air! Why do they not spontaneously combust even though the oxygen and the wood are always in contact with one another? The answer is activation energy.

Activation Energy

Activation energy was a concept devised by Svante Arrhenius. Simply put, it is the minimum amount of energy that must be added into a chemical reaction system that is needed for the reaction to start. The units of activation energy are KJ/mol. According to this principle, the Arrhenius equation was developed:

$$k = Ae^{-Ea/RT}$$

Where k is the reaction rate, A is a frequency factor based on each individual chemical reaction, Ea is the activation energy, R is the universal gas constant, and T is the temperature in degrees Kelvin. Based on this equation, there are two important concepts you need to understand:

1. For the majority of reactions, as temperature increases, the reaction rate increases.

2. As activation energy increases, reaction rate decreases.

Rate Law

The reaction rate law tells us which reactants are more important in a chemical reaction. This can be determined through experimentation. In an irreversible reaction where:

$$2A + B + C \rightarrow 2D$$

We get the following data:

Trial	A	B	C	Initial Reaction Rate
1	0.2	0.2	0.2	0.0004
2	0.4	0.2	0.2	0.0008
3	0.4	0.4	0.2	0.0016
4	0.2	0.2	0.4	0.0004

Based on this data, can we determine the importance of each reactant and the rate law?

From this experiment, the following information is obtained:

- Doubling the concentration of A doubles the reaction rate
- Doubling the concentration of A and B quadruples the reaction rate
- Doubling the concentration of C results in no change

The rate law can then be determined to be:

$$rate = k[A]^1[B]^1[C]^0$$

This is because increasing the concentrations of A and B lead to a linear increase of the reaction rate. If there were an exponential increase, A or B would have a power of 2 or 3, not 1. Increasing the concentration of reagent C results in absolutely no change. Thus, the concentration of C does not affect the rate, and has a rate exponent of 0.

The overall reaction rate of this equation is 2nd order. We can find the overall order of reaction by adding all the exponents seen in the rate equation.

Catalysis

There are some substances that are able to reduce the activation energy of a reaction, which subsequently will increase the reaction rate. There are two types of catalysts: biological and chemical.

Chemical Catalyst

A chemical catalyst is commonly a metal or other elemental compound with many electrons in their valence shell; they assist in the stabilization of reaction intermediates. Common chemical catalysts include platinum, palladium, nickel, or cobalt.

Biological Catalyst

A biological catalyst is known as an enzyme. Common enzymes include cellulase, amylase, or DNA polymerase. Biological catalysts typically function by bringing two reactants close together. Many enzymes also have active sites in their protein chains that function similarly to chemical catalyst, and assist in stabilizing reaction intermediates.

There are two types of catalysts subdivided by their phase: heterogeneous and homogenous:

- A heterogeneous catalyst is *not* in the same phase as the reactants. An example of a heterogeneous catalyst is the platinum found in the catalytic converter in the exhaust stream of cars. The catalyst is in the solid phase, and the reactants are in the gas phase.

- A homogenous catalyst is in the same phase as the reactants. Most enzymes are homogenous, and are soluble in the same phase as the reactants.

When a catalyst has been added to a reactant, there will be change in the energy diagram of the reaction, seen below:

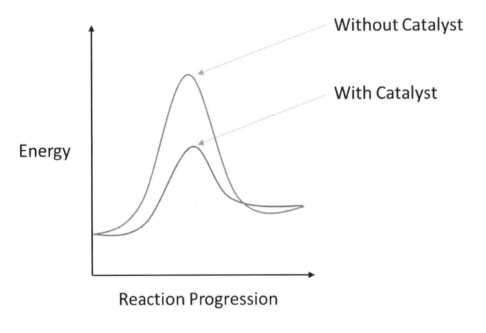

Figure 40

The primary action of the catalyst is to reduce the activation energy of the reaction. The starting and ending energy states remain the same. The activation energy barrier is lowered by the methods stated above: moving the reactants into close proximity with one another, or stabilizing the reaction intermediates.

Laws of Thermodynamics

Introduction

Thermodynamics is the study of energy in a system and its relationship to chemical reactions. The use of thermodynamics can help us understand the rate at which a reaction will occur, or whether or not a reaction will occur at all. There are three basic laws of thermodynamics:

The First Law

The internal energy of a system is equal to the heat in the system minus the work performed by the system.

$$U = Q - W$$

Where U is the internal energy, Q is the heat, and W is the work. This law can help us understand, for example, how much energy is present in a gas, and how much work a gas might produce. For example, the high temperature and pressure steam that passes through a turbine can produce work. The first law also demonstrates the conservation of energy.

This is probably the most important law for chemistry – it helps us understand energy in a system and how much energy needs to be placed into a system for a reaction to occur. For example, if the internal energy of a reactant is greater than the internal energy of the product, we know that energy must be released during the course of the reaction, either in the form of heat or work.

The Second Law

The entropy of a system increases with time and with action. In layman's terms, this law states that any action results in an increase of entropy, a property that describes disorder.

The Third Law

The entropy of a substance approaches zero as the temperature approaches absolute zero (0 Kelvin).

Endothermic and Exothermic Reactions

There are three types of reactions: endothermic, exothermic, and isothermic reactions. An endothermic reaction requires heat in order to proceed. An exothermic reaction releases heat during the course of the reaction. An isothermic reaction has no net input or output of energy. The type of reaction can be discerned from the reaction energy diagram, seen below:

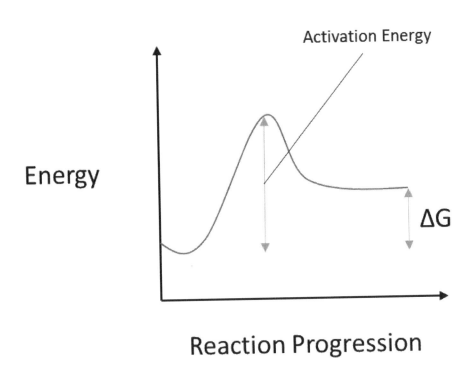

Figure 41

Gibb's Free Energy

In the reaction energy diagram, the reactants start at the left hand side of the graph. As the reaction progresses, energy needs to be added to the system or leave it.

As a result, the difference between the starting energy and the ending energy is the ΔG, or change in Gibb's Free Energy:

- If ΔG is positive, the reaction is endothermic

- If ΔG is negative, the reaction is exothermic

- If ΔG is 0, the reaction is isothermic

The chart above depicts an endothermic reaction. The energy state of the products is greater than that of the reactants, meaning the reaction requires energy. The two charts below represent reactions that are exothermic and isothermic, respectively.

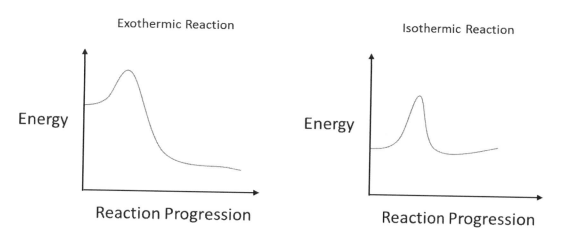

Figure 42

Heat, Energy, and Work

Heat, energy, and work are all defined by the joule, an SI unit that represents one Newton of force active over one second. One Newton is enough energy to accelerate 1 kg of mass at 1 m/s^2. The following equation is used to calculate kinetic energy:

$$K_e = \frac{1}{2}\, mv^2$$

Thus, the kinetic energy of a molecule or mass is equal to one half the mass multiplied by its velocity squared.

Heat Capacity & Calorimetry

The heat capacity of a substance is the amount of energy required to raise the temperature of the mass by a certain amount. The standard units for heat capacity are J/g*C, meaning the number of joules required to increase the temperature of one gram of material by one degree centigrade. It is also possible to express heat capacity using calories, or cal/g*C. The equation for heat capacity is:

$$q = m \times C\Delta T$$

Where q is the heat required, m is the mass, C is the heat capacity, and ΔT is the change in temperature. For example, the heat capacity (C) of water is 4.18 J/g*C. If 100g of water is heated from 25 °C to 100 °C, how much energy was required?

$$\Delta T = 100\text{-}25 = 75\ ^{\circ}C$$

$$C = 4.18\ J/g*C$$

$$q = 4.18\ J/g*C \times 100g \times 75^{\circ}C = 31{,}350\ \text{Joules}$$

The chemical experiment used to determine the heats of reactions based on the heat capacity of water or another compound is called the calorimeter. A calorimetry question is very likely to show up on the AP Chemistry exam. A calorimeter is a device that measures the energy change in a system, and is depicted on the next page:

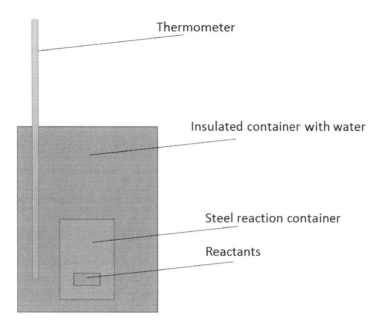

Figure: Bomb Calorimeter

Figure 43

In the calorimeter setup, the reactants are placed inside a steel reaction container submerged inside a container of water that is well insulated, for example by Styrofoam. As the reaction progresses, the water is either heated or cooled. Based on the temperature change of the water as measured by the thermometer, it is possible to determine the energy change, either exothermic or endothermic, that has occurred inside the reaction container.

On the AP Chemistry exam, there are two primary types of problems that involve thermodynamics. The first is a problem that involves reaction heats and/or heat capacity. This type of problem will test your ability to predict the amount of heat evolved in a reaction, and what the ending temperature of the reaction will be. The second type of problem involves a calorimeter. This type of problem will test your knowledge of the use of a calorimeter and assessment of data obtained in a calorimetry experiment.

Question: In the military, soldiers use small packets of chemical material that generate heat when exposed to water to heat food in the field. The reaction is:

$$Mg + 2H_2O \rightarrow Mg(OH)_2 + H_2 \text{ [+ heat]}$$

A soldier uses 100g of Mg in 1 liter of water, and the water temperature rises from 20 °C to 100 °C. What is the heat of reaction?

First, check to make sure the equation is balanced. In this case, it is! That makes things a lot easier. So let's look at the information we have:

- The reaction is known to produce heat. This means that it is an exothermic reaction, and the sign of our answer should be negative. ΔH is negative.

- The soldier heats 1 liter of water, which is 1000g. The heat capacity of water is known to be 4.18 J/g*K

- The soldier uses 100g of magnesium. We can calculate a molar mass from that.

Now, we calculate number of mols of reactant, and heat generated. Magnesium has a molar mass of 24.3 g/mol. Thus, 100g of magnesium is 4.12 mols.

The equation for heat capacity is:

$$q = m \times C\Delta T$$

Substitute our known values to find the heat generated, q.

$$q = 1000g \times 4.18\frac{J}{g \times K} \times 80\ C$$

$$q = 334,400\ Joules\ or\ 334.4\ kJ$$

Now, we can calculate the heat of the reaction and solve the problem. We know that 4.12 mols of magnesium was used. There is an excess of water, because 1000g of water is more than 50 mols of water.

Answer: The reaction heat is:

$$\Delta H = \frac{-334.4 \; kJ}{4.12 \; mols} = -81.16 \; kJ/mol$$

Question: A student is conducting an experiment in which he is burning a mixture of ethanol and methanol in a calorimeter. The calorimeter contains 500 mL of water. If the mixture of ethanol to methanol is a molar ratio of 60:40, and the water's temperature rising from 20 °C to 85 °C, what is the mass of ethanol that was used in the calorimeter?

Here are the equations for the burning of ethanol and methanol:

C_2H_5OH (l) + 3 O_2 (g) $\rightarrow$ 2 CO_2 (g) + 3 H_2O (liq); $-\Delta H_c$ = 1371 kJ/mol

2 CH_3OH (l) + 3 O_2(g) --> 2 CO_2 (g) + 4 H_2O (liq); $-\Delta H_c$ = 1079 kJ/mol

This is complicated, but no sweat. The important information in this problem is:

- We know the volume of water and the specific heat of water
- We know the mol ratio of ethanol to methanol in the calorimeter
- We've been given balanced equations, so this saves us a step.
- We've been given the heats of reaction of the chemical reactions.

Using the heat capacity equation, we find that the energy placed into the water is:

$$q = 500g \ \times 4.18 \frac{J}{g \times K} \times 65 \ C$$

$$q = 135.85 \ kJ$$

Using the ratio given in the problem, we calculate an average heat of reaction. If 60% is ethanol and 40% is methanol and 1 mol is burned, how much heat will be produced?

0.60 x 1371 kJ/mol + 0.40 x 1079 kJ/mol = 1254.2 kJ/mol

Great, so now we know that if we burn 1 mol of the ethanol methanol mixture, we will obtain 1254.2 kJ of energy. If 1 mol generates 1254.2 kJ of energy, and the energy released into the calorimeter is 135.85 kJ, we can see that:

$$mols = \frac{135.85 \ kJ}{1254.2 \ \frac{kJ}{mol}} = 0.108 \ mols$$

Now, we multiply that by 60% to get 0.0648 mols of ethanol.

Answer: The molecular weight of ethanol is 46 g/mol. This means that we have 2.98 (or just about 3) grams of ethanol in the calorimeter.

Again, the problems above are more challenging than you should expect on the AP Chemistry exam. However, if you understand the step by step methodology in analyzing and assessing these problems, the AP exam will be a breeze!

Laboratory

Design of Experiments & Laboratory Component

A critical part of the AP Chemistry Exam involves experiment design and understanding the chemical reactions performed in a lab. Students are expected to have performed the following experiments, and understand how to design an experiment and formulate a scientific hypothesis. If you haven't taken the AP Chemistry course, you'll want to pay extra special attention to this portion of the guide.

Design of an Experiment and Hypothesis

A scientific experiment is used to answer a particular question, which is formed by writing a hypothesis. The classic hypothesis is based on an "if/then" statement.

<u>If we perform action A, then we believe that result B will occur.</u>

For example, a written hypothesis could be: If we add sodium hydroxide to a solution of copper sulfate, then we believe that a precipitate will form. These are the basics, but there is far more that goes into writing a hypothesis. All hypotheses are based on a <u>premise</u>, which is prior knowledge that supports the hypothesis. *The premise establishes a relationship between the action and the conclusion.* For example, a poorly written hypothesis that does not have a strong premise is:

<u>If I walk under a ladder in the morning, I will have a stomachache after lunch.</u>

In this case, the premise is that walking under a ladder is connected to having stomach problems. This premise is not true, and thus the hypothesis or scientific question is invalid.

So let's start with a scientifically valid premise: the formation of a hydroxide compound with a metal is usually insoluble. Thus, we ask the question: Is the formation of copper hydroxide in a reaction solution insoluble? We can test this by writing the hypothesis and performing the experiment.

Common Experiments

Light Spectroscopy

Light spectroscopy measures the absorbance of visible light by a solution. The color present in a solution is indicative of the absorbance of a specific wavelength of light. The greater the absorbance, the darker the color appears, and this is correlated to the concentration of the solution.

Key Concepts

- The equation that relates absorptivity to concentration is the Beer-Lambert Law:

$$A = \varepsilon \times l \times c$$

   Where A is the absorptivity, e is the extinction coefficient, l is the path length the light is traveling through, and c is the concentration.

- The color of the solution corresponds to the wavelength that should be measured. For example, if a solution appears blue, it is absorbing light in the red to yellow wavelengths, between 550 and 700 nm.
- The experiment can be affected by impure solutions, light entering the spectroscopy area, and unclean cuvettes in the experiment.

On the exam, a question on light spectroscopy will often ask you to determine the results of an experiment based on the absorption of a solution.

Question: Iron (III) chloride is a compound that is sparingly soluble in hexane. A student collects a set of data on the concentration of iron in solution for a different amount of iron chloride added. The extinction coefficient was determined to be 0.8 and the path length is 1 cm. Calculate the concentration of the samples and plot a chart.

Sample	1	2	3	4
A	0.405	0.471	0.519	0.612
g/L	20	30	40	50

This problem is relatively straightforward. We can set up the equation for absorbance to solve for the concentration. The end result should be:

$$c = \frac{A}{\varepsilon \times l}$$

Using this equation, we can fill out the rest of the table:

Sample	1	2	3	4
A	0.405	0.471	0.519	0.612
g/L	20	30	40	50
C	0.506	0.588	0.649	0.765

Looking at the data, we can indeed conclude the iron (III) chloride is sparingly soluble in hexane. This makes sense because hexane is a non-polar solvent and iron chloride is an ionic (polar) compound. We can finish this problem off by making a small graph.

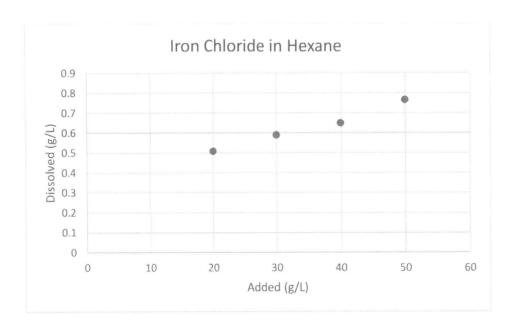

Titration

Titration is used to determine a solution's concentration by adding a neutralizing reagent. For example, if we have a concentration of 0.5M hydrochloric acid in solution, we would need to add a certain amount of strong base in order to fully neutralize the solution. The amount of base added can tell us exactly how much acid is in the solution.

Key Concepts

- *Equivalence point:* the point at which the chemical is completely neutralized is the equivalence point. It can be recognized on a titration chart as the point with the greatest slope.
- *Indicator:* an indicator is a substance that typically is able to change color in relationship to the concentration of the reagent we are using.

Here are some sample titration curves – the first is of a monoprotic acid.

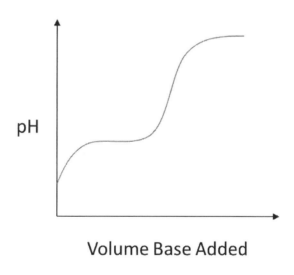

Volume Base Added

Figure 44

There is a dissociation of only a single proton, resulting in a steep slope at just one point in the curve.

This titration curve is for a diprotic acid, such as H_2SO_4.

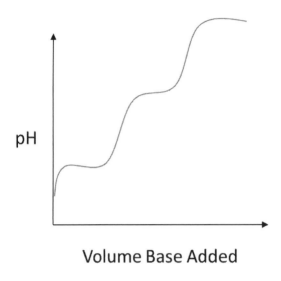

pH

Volume Base Added

Figure 45

Here, we can see that there are two bends in the graph, with two areas where there is a steep slope. This represents the dissociation of the first proton, followed by the second proton, respectively. You need to be able to identify from a titration chart the following information:

1. The number of protons an acid possesses

2. The half-equivalence point of each proton

3. The equivalence point of each proton

Reaction Rate

Experiments involving reaction rate are designed to assess the speed of a chemical reaction based on a set of parameters. Parameters commonly tested in lab are concentration and temperature. Other parameters that may affect the reaction rate, but cannot typically be tested in a classroom, are pressure and the presence of a catalyst.

A chemical reaction rate is normally expressed in the following units: mol/s, sometimes referred to as $mol*s^{-1}$. This is the number of mols of reactant consumed per second. A higher value indicates a faster reaction rate.

Reaction Extent & Ideal Gases

The reaction extent is the proportion to which the reactants have been consumed in the reaction. For example, a reaction extent of 0.9 indicates that 90% of reactants have been used. A common experiment used to show both the ideal gas law and reaction extent is the inflation of a balloon by sodium azide. Sodium azide is a compound found in airbags. When heated, it expands violently into sodium and nitrogen. The reaction is:

$$2\ NaN_3 \rightarrow 2\ Na + 3\ N_2\ (g)$$

In the laboratory experiment, you will be expected to be able to calculate the reaction extent of sodium azide based on the amount of gas in the balloon.

pH and Buffers

A buffer is a compound able to resist a change in pH. Buffers are usually made of an acid along with its conjugate base. The buffering capacity of a solution, which measures the total resistance of the solution to a change in pH, is governed by the pKa of the acid involved, as well as the ratio of the acid to its conjugate base. The buffering ability of a solution can be examined by the Hendersen-Hasselbach Equation, seen below:

$$pH = pKa + log_{10}\left(\frac{A-}{HA}\right)$$

Where pH is the pH of the solution, pKa is the pKa of the dissolved acid, A- is the conjugate base, and HA is the un-dissociated acid. Several important facts about buffers:

- Buffers <u>must</u> be composed of weak acids. Strong acids dissociate completely and are not good buffers.

- A buffer is only effective near the pH of its pKa. For example, the pKa of acetic acid is around 4.5. This means that acetic acid and its conjugate base is an effective buffer near the pH of 4.5. At much lower or much higher pH's, the acid will either be completely dissociated, leading to a log value that is much higher or much lower than expected, resulting in a net change of pH.

- Buffer strength depends on the concentration of the weak acid. A buffer solution of 1M will be able to tolerate the addition of about 0.5-1.0 M of other material that might change the pH. If more than that is added, then the buffer molecule will become "overwhelmed" and be unable to resist further pH changes.

Question: A student is making a buffer out of citric acid, which is a polyprotic acid. Explain how the student would make a buffer with a pH of 5 and describe the structure of the citric acid molecule at this pH.

Here are pKa values for citric acid (and its structure):

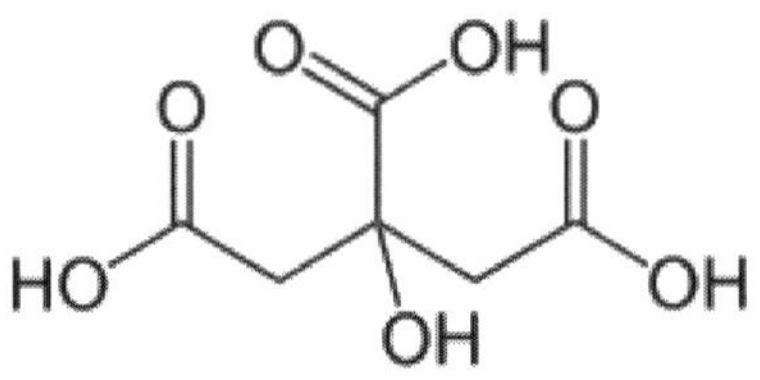

Figure 46

$$pK_{a1} = 3.14$$

$$pK_{a2} = 4.75$$

$$pK_{a3} = 6.39$$

It's clear that citric acid is a weak acid, with the pKa's given. It looks like there are three carboxylic acid (-COOH) functional groups on the molecule. Each one of these carboxylic acids is capable of donating a proton. As more protons are donated, the pKa increases, showing that the acidity of the 2nd and 3rd protons is lower than the first one. So we use the Hendersen-Hasselbach equation to evaluate it:

$$pH = pKa + log_{10}\left(\frac{A-}{HA}\right)$$

144

The first proton must be almost completely dissociated in order for the pH to be 5. We can check this:

$$5 = 3.14 + log_{10}\left(\frac{A-}{HA}\right)$$

In order for the pH to be 5, the ratio of conjugate base to un-dissociated acid needs to be at least 100:1 to produce a log value of 2. This means that we are now dealing with the second proton. We substitute the value of pKa for the second proton into the equation and take a look.

$$5 = 4.75 + log_{10}\left(\frac{A-}{HA}\right)$$

This is more promising. For the second proton's pH to be 5, we see that log (A-/HA) needs to be roughly 2:1, meaning 66% of the second proton needs to be dissociated. (Note log(2) = 0.30)

Answer: In order to make a buffer with a pH of 5, the student will need to add citric acid to solution, and then adjust the pH to 5 with a base. In this manner, the first proton in citric acid will be forced to dissociate to counteract the base. If no base is added, then the pH of citric acid by itself in water will be close to its pKa, or 3.14.

At a pH of 5, the structure of the citric acid will have completely lost its first proton and will have a negative charge. The buffer at a pH of 5 is maintained by the second acidic proton on the structure and its conjugate base. According to the Hendersen-Hasselbach equation, approximately 66% of the second proton needs to be dissociated before a pH of 5 can be reached. Thus, 66% of the citric acid molecules in this solution will have just a single proton remaining, while 33% of the molecules will have 2 protons remaining.

Practice Examination

Practice Examination 1

Multiple Choice Questions

1. Assuming a non-ionized hydrogen atom, which of these electron transitions' spectral lines in the associated emission spectrum would have the longest wavelength?

   a) Level 3 → Level 2

   b) Level 4 → Level 3

   c) Level 4 → Level 2

   d) All electron transitions would have the same wavelength spectral line

Questions 2-4 refer to the following titration curve for 30 mL of a hypothetical acid titrated with 0.1M NaOH.

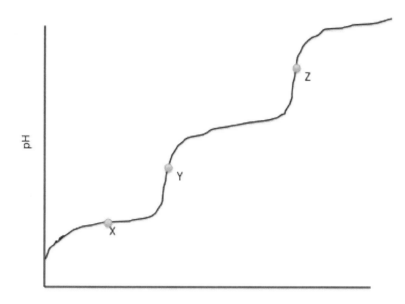

Volume NaOH

2. Which of the following best explains the shape of the curve?

   a) The acid is amphoteric.

   b) The acid is polyprotic.

   c) The reaction of the acid with the base is a double replacement reaction

   d) The acid is acting as an electron pair donor.

3. Which of these statements is true about point X on the graph?

a) There is excess base present.

b) There is an equivalent amount of fully protonated acid and partially deprotonated acid.

c) There is an equivalent amount of partially deprotonated acid and fully deprotonated acid.

d) There is more fully deprotonated acid than partially deprotonated acid present.

4. The volume of NaOH used at Point Y is 12 mL and the volume at Point Z is 24 mL. What is the concentration of the unknown acid?

a) 0.1 M

b) 0.04 M

c) 0.08 M

d) There is not information to determine this.

5. A man on a partially depressurized airline flight (720 mm Hg) with a cabin temperature of 22ºC finishes drinking a disposable plastic 0.5L water bottle and puts the cap back on. When he disembarks at the airport where the pressure is 1 atm and the temperature is 24ºC, what will happen to the volume of his empty bottle?

a) It will increase.

b) It will decrease.

c) It will remain the same.

d) There is not enough information to determine what will happen.

6. Which of these methods would be the best to experimentally determine the identity of an unknown anion?

a) Place a clean wire coated in analyte solution in the flame of a Bunsen burner to determine the color of flame produced.

b) Test for the formation of a precipitate in the presence of particular metal salts.

c) Titrate the anion with a strong base.

d) Analyze the absorption/transmission of a series of dilutions of the analyte at a single wavelength in a spectrophotometer.

7. Which of these processes is exothermic?

   a)   Freezing ice cubes.

   b)   Baking a cake.

   c)   Melting iron.

   d)   Breaking up a gaseous diatom.

8. Iron is often coated with other metals for manufacturing and industrial purposes. If a piece of iron that was treated with a layer of zinc is scratched to expose the iron to the air, it will corrode, but not as quickly as a piece of iron that was treated with a layer of tin that gets scratched – in this case, the exposed iron becomes rusty even faster than it would if it were never coated at all. From this we can deduce:

   a)   Zinc is the most reactive of these metals

   b)   Tin is the most reactive of these metals

   c)   Iron is the least reactive of these metals.

   d)   Iron is the most reactive of these metals.

9. 32 grams of an unknown metal are heated from 20ºC to 95ºC. This process requires 2000 Joules of energy. This tells us that:

   a)   The heat capacity of the metal is 1.2

   b)   The heat capacity of the metal is 0.83

   c)   The specific heat of the metal is 0.83

   d)   The specific heat of the metal is 1.2

10. Which of these chemical structures would not have a dipole?

   a)   Bent molecule with one pair of unshared electrons on the central atom.

   b)   Bent molecule with two pairs of unshared electrons on the central atom.

   c)   Square planar molecule with two pairs of unshared electrons on the central atom.

   d)   Trigonal planar molecule with one pair of unshared electrons on the central atom.

11. Which of these molecular shapes describes the structure of ammonia?

a) Tetrahedral

b) Bent

c) Trigonal planar

d) Trigonal pyramidal

12. Which of these statements is not true of covalent bonds?

a) They include two overlapping atomic orbitals.

b) The net formal charge on the resulting compound must be zero.

c) They allow bonded atoms to achieve electron configurations comparable to those of noble gases.

d) They may include more than one pair of shared electrons.

13. What type of covalent bonds would be found in CO_2?

a) Two sigma bonds and two pi bonds

b) Four sigma bonds

c) One pi bond and three sigma bonds

d) One sigma bond and three pi bonds

14. Which of these is not a properly named chemical by ionic nomenclature?

a) Potassium acetate

b) Lithium hydroxide

c) Lead nitrate

d) Calcium sulfite

15. Which of the lines in the graph below would you expect to match the absorption pattern of a blue dye?

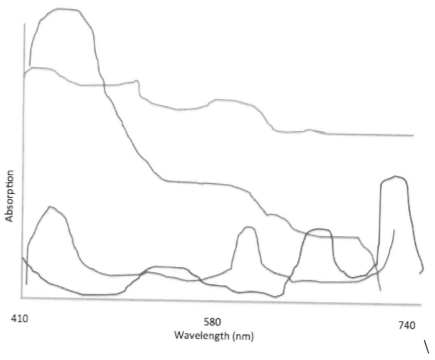

a) Green

b) Red

c) Purple

d) Blue

16. A chemical reaction has a positive change in enthalpy and a positive change in entropy. Based on this, under what circumstances would the reaction be expected to be spontaneous?

a) All temperatures

b) High temperatures only

c) Low temperatures only

d) The reaction would never be spontaneous

17. Which of these processes would be expected to be entropically favorable?

a) The conversion of nitrogen dioxide to dinitrogen tetroxide

b) The condensation of water vapor into liquid water

c) The combination of carbon and hydrogen gas to form methane.

d) The dissolving of sodium nitrate in water.

18. Which of these findings best demonstrates the electron-shell (Rutherford-Bohr) model of the atom?

a) The spectra shown when an atom emits an electron include only certain specific wavelengths of light and not the entire range of available frequencies.

b) A thin gold foil sheet bombarded with subatomic particles will mostly allow those particles through unimpeded, but occasionally deflect one back in the direction it was fired.

c) The reaction of two gases in a closed container to form a third gas does not alter the mass of the container and its contents.

d) Under neutron bombardment, uranium decays into barium.

19. The element Unknownium has a small atomic radius and a high ionization energy compared to other elements of comparable atomic mass. This element is most likely to be a:

a) Alkali metal

b) Halogen

c) Transition metal

d) Alkaline earth metal

20. If light has a frequency of 220 nm, what is its energy in Joules?

a) $x \ 10^{-7}$

b) $x \ 10^{15}$

c) $x \ 10^{-15}$

d) 9.0×10^{-19}

Questions 21-24 regard the combustion of cinnamic acid, an organic compound composed of carbon, hydrogen, and oxygen.

21. If an 8.7 gram sample of cinnamic acid is completely combusted to yield 23.27 g of carbon dioxide and 4.23 g of water, what is the empirical formula of cinnamic acid?

a) CHO

b) $C_2H_2O_5$

c) $C_9H_8O_2$

d) C_4H_4O

22. Under what conditions could the empirical formula for cinnamic acid from the given experimental data be incorrect?

a) The reaction occurred under greater than normal atmospheric pressure

b) The reaction chamber did not contain an excess of oxygen

c) The reaction chamber was composed of glass rather than nonreactive metal

d) Cinnamic acid contains a double bond

23. What would be a good way to determine the ΔH of the described reaction?

a) Conduct the reaction in a bomb calorimeter

b) Affix a thermometer to the outside of the reaction chamber

c) Analyze a sample of cinnamic acid in a mass spectrometer

d) Combust the cinnamic acid in the presence of an indicator

24. Which of the following statements would you expect to be true of the described reaction?

a) It does not require activation energy.

b) It has a negative enthalpy of reaction.

c) It gives a net loss of entropy.

d) It is endothermic.

25. Which of the following is not true of the alkali metals?

a) They are more likely to be oxidized than reduced.

b) They typically form +1 monatomic cations.

c) It requires a lot of energy to remove an electron from the outermost occupied .

d) They are highly reactive.

26. In organic biomolecules such as proteins and DNA, a great deal of secondary structure is provided between interactions between the constituent pieces of the chain – while these bonds are fairly strong, they frequently break to permit the molecule to bend and flex. The described interactions are most likely caused by:

a) Hydrogen bonding

b) Ionic bonding

c) Covalent bonding

d) van der Waals forces

27. Which of the following molecules would be expected to dissolve best in water?

a) Propane

b) Isobutanol

c) Octene

d) Benzoic acid

28. An unknown solid substance is found to conduct electricity poorly. A good next step to determine whether this is an ionic or covalent compound would be to:

a) Find its melting point

b) Test its conductivity when dissolved in water

c) Test its flammability

d) Find its density.

Questions 29-31 deal with the following graphs. The concentration of reactant [A] was measured over time as the reaction proceeded and yielded the following data.

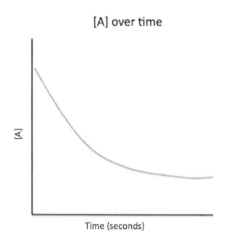

[A] over time

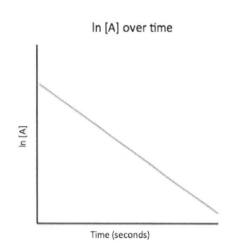

ln [A] over time

29. Which of these must be true of the reaction rate?

    a) It is a zero order reaction

    b) It is a first order reaction

    c) It is a second order reaction

    d) The order cannot be determined from this data.

30. What would happen if more of reactant A were added to the reaction chamber?

    a) The rate of reaction would increase.

    b) The rate of reaction would decrease.

    c) The rate of reaction would stay the same.

    d) The equilibrium of the reaction would shift toward formation of A rather than of P.

31. The reaction described by these graphs could be:

a) A biomolecule synthesis that only occurs in the presence of a necessary enzyme.

b) The isomerization of an organic compound.

c) The combustion of gasoline.

d) The reaction of calcium carbonate with hydrochloric acid to form water, carbon dioxide, and calcium chloride.

32. An ice cube left out in a glass at room temperature will eventually melt and reach equilibrium with its environment. This best demonstrates the principle that:

a) There is no net creation or destruction of energy in a chemical reaction.

b) Systems tend to progress toward disorder over time.

c) Enthalpy is a dominant force over entropy in determining spontaneity of ions.

d) Temperature is a measure of the average kinetic motion of particles.

Questions 33-36 refer to the following graph.

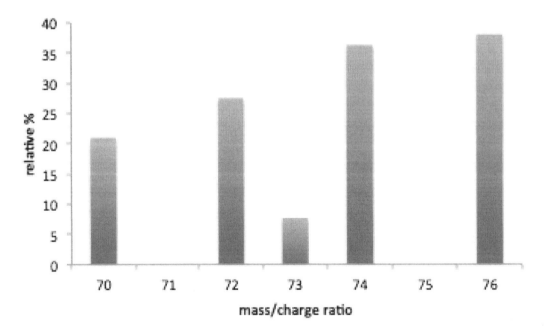

33. This data appears to have been collected using the technique of:

a) Nuclear magnetic resonance

b) Titration

c) Crystallography

d) Mass spectroscopy

34. The element analyzed in this experiment is:

a) Hafnium

b) Germanium

c) Osmium

d) Calcium

35. Experiments of this type show that which part of Dalton's model of the atom is inaccurate?

a) Elements are composed of particles called atoms.

b) Any two atoms of a specific element are indistinguishable.

c) Atoms of different elements can be combined to form compounds.

d) Atoms cannot be created nor destroyed in chemical reactions.

36. Which of the peaks in the graph represents the form of the element with the most protons?

a) The peak at 70.

b) The peak at 76.

c) The peak at 73.

d) They would all have the same number of protons.

Questions 37-39 refer to the following experimental data: 50 mL of an aqueous solution of silver nitrate of unknown concentration is mixed with an aqueous solution of calcium chloride. A precipitate forms and is collected via gravimetric analysis. After drying, 1.3 grams of solid remain.

37. What is the precipitate?

a) Silver chloride

b) Calcium nitrate

c) Excess calcium chloride

d) Excess silver nitrate

38. How can we ensure that silver nitrate is the limiting reagent?

a) Add a larger volume of calcium chloride than of silver nitrate

b) Warm the beaker where the mixture occurs

c) Add calcium chloride until no more precipitate forms

d) Avoid stirring or mixing the beaker while the reaction is occurring.

39. Assuming all of the silver nitrate reacts, what is the concentration of the original silver nitrate solution?

a) 0.09 M

b) 0.18 M

c) 0.36 M

d) 1.5 M

40. Which of these is not a demonstration of colligative properties?

a) Salting the water before making pasta will allow it to boil slightly faster.

b) Slices of raw potato will lose mass when soaked in a concentrated sugar solution, ain mass when soaked in pure water.

c) Hot and cold water poured into the same glass will eventually equilibrate to an even temperature.

d) A purer gasoline is less resistant to catching fire than a gasoline that contains more contaminants.

Questions 41-43 refer to the following table.

Acid	K_a (mol·dm^{-3})
H_2S	8.9×10^{-8}
HF	5.6×10^{-4}
CH_3COOH	1.7×10^{-5}

41. Which of these acids would you expect dissociates the least effectively when dissolved in water?

    a) H_2S

    b) HF

    c) CH_3COOH

    d) It cannot be determined from this information

42. In a 0.8 M solution of HF, what would be the pH?

    a) 0.021

    b) 1.7

    c) 3.25

    d) 4

43. Which of the acids in the table has a pKa of 7.1?

    a) H_2S

    b) HF

    c) CH_3COOH

    d) It cannot be determined without knowing the solution's molarity.

Questions 44-46 refer to the following chemical equation:

$$2Fe_{(s)} + 3Cl_{2\ (g)} \rightarrow 2FeCl_{3\ (s)}$$
$$Fe^{3+} + 3\,e^- \rightarrow Fe_{(s)} \qquad E^0 = -0.04$$
$$Cl_2\,(g) + 2\,e^- \rightarrow 2\,Cl^- \qquad E^0 = 1.36$$

44. Assuming a standard state, what is the cell potential for this reaction?

   a) 4.00 V

   b) -4.00 V

   c) 1.4 V

   d) -1.4 V

45. Is this a spontaneous reaction?

   a) Yes

   b) No

   c) It cannot be determined without knowing the value for ΔS

   d) It cannot be determined without knowing the value for both ΔS and ΔH

46. Which of these shows a balanced net ionic equation?

   a) $H^+_{(aq)} + Cl^-_{(aq)} + Na^+_{(aq)} + OH^-_{(aq)} \rightarrow H2O_{(l)} + NaCl_{(aq)}$

   b) $PO_4^{3-}{}_{(aq)} + Ca^{2+}{}_{(aq)} \longrightarrow Ca_3(PO_4)_{2\ (s)}$

   c) $Zn_{(s)} + Cu^{2+}{}_{(aq)} + SO_4^{2-}{}_{(aq)} \longrightarrow Zn^{2+}{}_{(aq)} + SO_4^{2-}{}_{(aq)} + Cu_{(s)}$

   d) $Ca^{2+}{}_{(aq)} + 2\,Cl^-_{(aq)} + 2\,Ag^+_{(aq)} + 2\,NO_3^-{}_{(aq)} \rightarrow Ca^{2+}{}_{(aq)} + 2\,NO_3^-{}_{(aq)} + 2\,AgCl_{(s)}$

47. At 35ºC and standard pressure, what will be the volume occupied by a 25.0-gram sample of methane gas?

   a) 632 L

   b) 4.48 L

   c) 71.8 L

   d) 39.4 L

48. At STP, a sample of an unknown gas occupies 40.0 L and weighs 50.1 grams. What is the identity of this gas?

a) carbon dioxide

b) nitrogen

c) nitrous oxide

d) butane

49. A balloon is filled with a mixture of 5.1 grams carbon dioxide and 6.7 grams nitrogen gas. The balloon is then placed in a bell jar and depressurized to 0.5 atm. What is the partial pressure of the carbon dioxide in the balloon?

a) 0.38 atm

b) 0.17 atm

c) atm

d) 1.5 atm

50. Which of these statements about solubility is not true?

a) The carbonation of a can of soda decreases if it is left in a warm car.

b) Ionic compounds are typically insoluble in nonpolar solvents.

c) A solution of potassium chloride that is saturated at room temperature will e super-saturated at 37ºC.

d) The solubility of nitrogen gas in water can be increased by increasing the proportion of nitrogen in the atmosphere above the surface of the solvent.

51. The K_{sp} of magnesium hydroxide is 5.61×10^{-12}. How many grams of magnesium hydroxide will dissolve in 100 mL of water?

a) 0.00081 g

b) 0.0011 g

c) 9.9×10^{-6} g

d) 1.38×10^{-5} g

52. Which of these descriptions is not characteristic of the quantum model of the atom?

  a) No two electrons in an orbital can occupy the same state simultaneously.

  b) Energy exists in discrete packets called photons.

  c) Electron orbits can be described in terms of spherical shells.

  d) Certain types of matter such as electrons exhibit properties normally associated with waves.

53. Which of these is the correct electron configuration for gold?

  a) [Xe] 6s2 5d9

  b) [Xe] 5d9 6s2

  c) [Xe] 4f14 5d10 6s1

  d) [Xe] 6s2 5d10 4f13

Questions 54-55 refer to a solution of 6.0 grams of hypochlorous acid dissolved in 250 mL water. (T = 25ºC, $K_a = 2.9 \times 10^{-8}$)

54. What is the concentration of hydroxide ions in this solution?

  a) 0.46 M

  b) 1.2×10^{-4} M

  c) 8.7×10^{-11} M

  d) It cannot be determined without the K_w for this acid.

55. What is the pH of the described solution?

  a) 3.9

  b) 10.1

  c) 7.5

  d) 0.33

56. Assume a hypothetical enzyme-catalyzed reaction where reactant A is modified to create product B. Which of these graphs best models the rate of reaction given that there is no new source of A during the reaction?

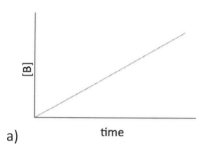

a)

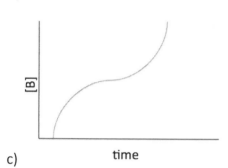

b)

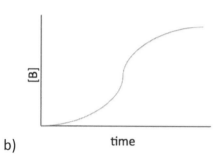

c)

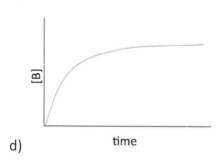

d)

57. A hypothetical chemical reaction has the rate law expression R = k[reactant]^2. What will happen to the rate of the reaction if the concentration of the reactant is halved?

a) The reaction rate will double.

b) The reaction rate will quadruple.

c) The reaction rate will be halved.

d) The reaction rate will be ¼ the original rate.

58. Which of these statements about hydrochloric acid is not true?

a) It will completely dissociate to its component ions when dissolved in water.

b) It can only be neutralized by a strong base, not a weak base.

c) It has a very large K_a.

d) It acts as a Brønsted acid.

59. Which of these gases would have the most rapid rate of effusion?

a) nitrous oxide

b) argon

c) oxygen

d) methane

60. Which of these properties of water does not arise from its hydrogen bonding?

a) Frozen water (ice) is less dense than liquid water.

b) Water behaves as a buffer, donating H+ or OH- ions as needed.

c) Water has strong surface tension.

d) Water is resistant to increases in temperature.

Free Response

1. **Magnesium combusts in the presence of oxygen. Use the following experimental data to answer the questions below. (10 pts)**

Table A: Magnesium metal mixed with hydrochloric acid

Mass of Mg metal (g)	Volume of 1M HCl (mL)	Initial temperature ($^\circ$C)	Final temperature ($^\circ$C)
0.2 g	100 mL	22.0°C	32.5°C

Table B: Magnesium oxide mixed with hydrochloric acid

Mass of magnesium oxide	Volume of 1M HCl (mL)	Initial temperature ($^\circ$C)	Final temperature ($^\circ$C)
1.0	100 mL	22.0°C	29.4°C

(a.) Describe and explain the experimental design in which data of this type might be collected and describe possible sources of error. (2 pts)

(b.) Write the balanced equation for the combustion of magnesium. (2 pts)

(c.) Calculate the enthalpy for the change in enthalpy for the reaction in part (b.) using the experimental data. You can assume a specific heat of 4.18 J/g·°C for all solutions, and that the enthalpy for the reaction of hydrogen and oxygen gas to form water is -259 kJ/mol. (4 pts)

(d.) Is this reaction exothermic or endothermic? Explain. (2 pts)

2. (a.) Describe two conditions under which the behavior of real gases is not well modeled by the behavior of ideal gases, the reason for this difference, and the effect of each incorrect assumption on calculations of volume made using the Combined Gas Law. (6 pts)

(b.) An equal number of moles of oxygen and nitrogen gas are mixed, and this mixture weighs a total of 20 grams. Assuming ideal gas behavior, what is the density of the gas at 350 K and 1 atm? (4 pts)

3. Nitric oxide reacts with hydrogen gas to form nitrogen gas and water.

   (a.) Write a balanced equation for this reaction. (2 pts)

   (b.) Using the below experimental data, write a complete rate expression including correct exponents and rate constant in its proper units for this reaction. (6 pts)

   (c.) Propose two means by which the equilibrium in this reaction could be shifted in favor of the products (2 pts).

Initial [NO]	Initial [H_2]	Initial rate of reaction in M/min
0.050	0.050	0.0040
0.10	0.15	0.0120
0.050	0.10	0.0080

4. Which of these would have the least effect on the freezing point of water? Give mathematical proof of your answer, and give the new freezing point. K_f water = 1.86 °C kg/mol (4 pts)

   - 0.10 m $C_{12}H_{22}O_{11}$

   - 0.20 m NaCl

   - 0.15 m $MgCl_2$

5. (a.) Which of these would you expect to have a stronger ionic bond: NaCl, KCl, or CsCl? Explain your reasoning. (2 pts)

(b.) Which of these would you expect to be most soluble in water: NaF, NaCl, or NaBr? Explain your reasoning. (2 pts)

6. (a.) Draw Lewis dot diagrams for nitrate ion and ammonia. (2 pts)

(b.) Identify the molecular shape of each and explain why they have different shapes. (2 pts)

7. Nitric acid reacts with arsenious acid to form nitric oxide, arsenic acid, and water.

(a.) Write the balanced equation for this reaction. (1 pt)

(b.) Describe three ways to increase the rate of formation of the products of this reaction and explain the mechanism of action. (3 pts)

Answer Key 1

Multiple Choice Answers

1. **a)**

   Because electrons have lower energy in lower orbitals, this is the lowest-energy transition and so would have the longest (and therefore most low energy) wavelength, one in the red spectrum.

   b) has the electron starting from a higher-energy position, and c) has a two-level jump, both of which would have a higher-energy, shorter-wavelength emission, so these answers are incorrect. The emission wavelength depends on the initial and final position of the electron, so d) is also incorrect.

2. **b)**

   The acid is diprotic: the two equivalent points in the graph represent the two deprotonations of this acid.

   a) is incorrect because while the acid may or may not be amphoteric, it will act as a proton donor/electron pair accepter if in the presence of a strong base such as NaOH. c) is not correct, as the type of reaction is irrelevant to the shape of the titration curve (most acid-base reactions are double replacement), and d) is not correct; acids do not act as electron pair donors.

3. **b)**

   Point X represents the midway point to the first equivalence; here, half of the acid is represented is in the form H2A, and half is in the form HA-.

   a) is incorrect as there will not be excess base until the rightmost portion of the graph; c) is incorrect, as there will not be equivalent amounts of fully and partially deprotonated acid until the next midway point. d) will only be true following the next midway point.

4. d)

Without knowing if the K_a of the first and second deprotonations are well separated, we cannot tell how much of the NaOH being used up to each equivalent point is reacting with the fully protonated species of the acid compared to the partially deprotonated version.

a) is the concentration of the base, which is unrelated to that of the acid; b) is incorrect but would be the right answer if we knew that the two K_a's were well separated and c) is the incorrect answer you would find if you used the total NaOH used up to the second equivalence point rather than the subtotal for either equivalence point.

5. b)

While the temperature increases, the pressure does too, which have opposite effects on the volume of a container. We must use the Combined Gas Law to find which, if either, has the greater effect.

1 atm is equivalent to 760 mm Hg, so we can substitute that into Combined Gas Law; we also need to convert temperature to Kelvins.

(P1 x V1)/T1 = (P2 x V2)/T2

(720 * 0.5)/293.15 = (760 * V2)/295.15

1.23 = 2.57*V2

1.23/2.57 = 2.57*V2/2.57

V2 = 0.48 L

So the volume has decreased.

6. b)

The results will help to place the anion in the known hierarchy of reactivity.

a) is a good method to detect cations based on characteristic emission colors, but does not work for anions, as when heated to become a gas, they are losing electrons to return to their neutral state rather than gaining them; this requires energy rather than inputting energy that may be emitted as colored light as is the case with cations. c) can help to find the concentration of the substance but not its identity, as is the case with d) – analyzing the entire absorption spectrum of a substance could be a valid experimental design but a single wavelength will not be helpful.

7. a)

As water freezes into ice, chemical bonds form and energy is released.

b), c), and d) require input of energy to occur, making these three choices endothermic and incorrect.

8. a)

The iron does not corrode as quickly because the zinc reacts more readily with the atmospheric oxygen, whereas this is not the case with tin.

b) is incorrect as tin must be the least reactive of these metals; which makes c) and d) incorrect as well.

9. c)

the specific heat of a substance describes how much energy is required to raise 1 gram of that substance 1ºC in temperature; we can find this number by dividing the given number of joules by the mass times the change in temperature:

S = 2000 / (32 x 75) = 0.83

The specific heat capacity, in contrast, is a quantity that takes into account both the amount of a substance as well as the specific heat and can be found by multiplying the mass by the specific heat. In this case the heat capacity would be 26.56.

10. c)

The symmetrical nature of the molecule (the two unshared pairs are oriented opposite one another and cancel each other out) means it cannot have a dipole.

The other three answers are asymmetrical and have one or more pairs of non-opposing electron pairs that act as a dipole.

11. d)

The unbounded electron pair on the nitrogen atom repels the electrons in the nitrogen-hydrogen bonds.

a) is not correct because the unbonded orbital is not included in the orbital shape, only the three that are bonded; there are too many atoms for a bent shape, so b) is incorrect; and c) is not right because the unbonded pair prevents a flat planar shape.

12. b)

Covalent molecules can include ions such as sulfate (SO_4^{2-}).

Covalent bonds are by definition the overlap of orbitals between two atoms so that they may achieve lower-energy electron configurations, like those of the noble gases, making a) and c) incorrect. Double and triple bonds include more than one pair of shared electrons, making d) incorrect.

13. a)

There are two sigma bonds, one from the carbon to each oxygen, and then a pi bond in addition – a double bond always consists of one sigma and one pi bond.

14. c)

Lead nitrate is not properly named, since lead is a transition metal that can have more than one possible charge, which must be specified in the name (for example, lead (II) nitrate).

15. b)

The red line has no peak in the violet/blue region of the spectrum because the blue light is what is being reflected. The absorption peaks toward the long end of the spectrum mean that these orange/red wavelengths are being absorbed at a higher rate.

The other lines all feature peaks in the blue region of the graph, which would indicate that this color of light is being absorbed rather than reflected.

16. b)

While the enthalpy change is unfavorable, in the equation $\Delta G = \Delta H - T\Delta S$, a large value for T magnifies the effect of the favorable entropy.

Therefore a) and c) are wrong – at low temperatures, the entropy benefits cannot overcome the enthalpy; and d) is wrong because at high temperatures the entropy change will matter more than the enthalpy change.

17. d)

When dissolved in water, the sodium and nitrate ions will dissociate, and increase the number of particles, increasing the entropy.

a) is incorrect because a new additional chemical bond is created from the lone electrons on the nitrogen central atoms of the nitrogen dioxide to create a single, larger molecule in place of two smaller ones – a more ordered system. b) represents a loss of entropy as liquid is a more ordered state than gas. c), similar to a), increases the number of bonds and decreases the number of particles.

18. a)

Because an electron can only exist at specific energy levels and must move between these, there are discrete amounts of energy released with each move, and each amount of energy is associated with a particular wavelength. An electron can move from level 3 to level 2, but it cannot move to level "2.5", so any frequencies associated with such intermediate jumps cannot ever be shown in the emission spectrum.

b) is an experiment that proves most of the mass of an atom is concentrated (in its nucleus) but does not speak to the arrangement of electrons. c) is a demonstration of the conservation of mass and d) is a demonstration of nuclear fission.

19. b)

Atomic radius tends to decrease toward the right hand side of the periodic table, as the increased number of protons in the nucleus exerts a stronger attractive force on the electrons in the outermost shell.

a), c), and d) all have fewer protons than comparable elements in their periods and so are not likely to match the given description.

20. d)

By plugging the given information into the equation $c = \lambda v$, we can find that $v = 1.36 \times 10^{15}$ s^{-1}. That value can then be used in the equation $E = hv$, along with Planck's constant, to find that $E = 9 \times 10^{-19}$ J.

21. c)

To find the number of moles of each element that reacted, we must start from the number of moles of each product produced and work backwards to find their original mass.

Carbon

23.27 g carbon dioxide * (1 mol carbon dioxide / 44 g carbon dioxide) = 0.53 mol CO_2 = 0.53 mol carbon

.53 mol C * (12 g / 1 mol) = 6.36

Hydrogen:

4.23 g water * (1 mol water / 18 g water) * (2 mol H / 1 mol H20) = 0.470 mol H

.470 mol H * (1 g H / 1 mol H) = .470 g H

Oxygen

Some of the oxygen in the reaction came from the cinnamic acid and some from the air. To find the amount from the acid alone, subtract the mass of the carbon and hydrogen from the original mass of the reactant.

8.7 – 6.36 - .470 = 1.87 g O

Then convert that to moles of O:

1.87 g O * (1 mol O / 16 g O) = 0.12 mol O

That gives us a molar ratio of:

.53 C : .47 H : 0.12 O

So if we divide each quantity by the smallest number of moles (0.12), we find:

4.4 C : 4 H : 1 O

Doubling this to give us whole numbers, we find $C_9H_8O_2$.

a) and d) are simply wrong answers, but b) is the wrong answer you would get if you failed to consider the oxygen being added to the reaction that did not come from the cinnamic acid.

22. b)

If there were not enough oxygen, the cinnamic acid would fail to combust completely and the measured amount of products would not reflect the full molar quantity of reactants.

a) and c) are incorrect as the atmospheric pressure and type of chamber material (assuming non-reactivity) would not affect the quantity of products. d) is incorrect because even though cinnamic acid does contain several double bonds, the types of bonds present are accounted for in the calculations of how many atoms of each element are present: whether two carbons are singly or double bonded in the reactant, they will still yield two carbon atoms in the products.

23. a)

This will allow you to measure the total heat flow over time.

For b), some heat may be lost to the outside environment and would cause incorrect calculations. c) would help to identify the structure of cinnamic acid but is unsuitable for finding the change in enthalpy, and d) is not a helpful experimental design.

24. b)

Combustion reactions by definition produce heat as a product, and this release of energy corresponds to a decrease in enthalpy.

a) is incorrect as even spontaneous reactions require a certain energy level to proceed. c) is incorrect because the conversion of high-energy complex molecules to simpler gases represents a gain in entropy. d) is incorrect because the reaction is a combustion and must produce heat.

25. c)

The alkali metals have the lowest ionization energy of their respective periods.

a) is incorrect, as these metals are likely to be oxidized (lose electrons), b) is incorrect because the loss of the outermost electron leaves the metal with a +1 charge, making it a cation, and d) is incorrect because this property does in fact make them highly reactive.

26. a)

Hydrogen bonds are weaker than covalent bonds, but stronger than van der Walls, and they are found in organic molecules where ionic bonds would not be.

27. b)

The alcohol side chain makes the molecule polar and therefore soluble in water.

a) and c) are plain hydrocarbon chains and so are nonpolar and insoluble; d) is a large organic acid, which are weak acids that do not dissociate strongly in water, so while it would dissolve better than propane or octane it would not do as well as isobutanol.

28. b)

While ionic solids conduct electricity when broken apart into their component ions in water, covalent compounds still fail to conduct electricity well in this state.

a) and d) are not helpful because ionic compounds have a wide range of melting points, and both types of compound have a variety of densities. Many substances of both types are flammable, so c) does not help.

29. b)

The graph of [A] is curved and the graph of ln [A] is straight, indicating that this is a first order reaction. If the first graph was straight and the second were curved a) would be correct, and if both graphs were curved c) would be correct.

30. a)

Because this is a first order reaction, the rate depends on the concentration of the reactant, and increasing the reactant will correspondingly increase the rate.

b) and d) are wrong, as more reactant will increase the rate and shift the equilibrium's stress in favor of the product. c) is wrong, because this is not a zero order reaction.

31. b)

It is a single-reactant reaction.

a) describes a zero-order reaction because the necessity of the enzyme means the reaction rate will not depend on the concentration of the reactants but rather enzyme availability. c) and d) depend on multiple reactants and describe second order reactions.

32. b)

The equilibration of the ice cube represents a loss of order: the cold molecules "sorted" into the ice cube compared to the warmer molecules in the rest of the room. When the entire room including the ice/water has reached an intermediate temperature, this order is gone.

a) is a description of the first law of thermodynamics, but no chemical reaction has occurred here. c) is only true depending on the temperature of a reaction, and in this case both the entropy and enthalpy changes would be favorable. d) is true but this demonstration does not show that this is so.

33. d)

This is the sort of data you would see from a mass spectrometer.

34. b)

The only possible answer is Germanium, which has an atomic mass of 72.61.

a) and c) have atomic numbers of 72 and 76 respectively, but this experiment is showing the relative abundance of each mass, not of different numbers of protons.

35. b)

The various isotopes represented in the experimental data show that individual atoms of the same element may differ in the number of neutrons present. The other three statements are accurate.

36. d)

The atoms would vary in the number of neutrons, not protons, or they would be from different elements; so the first three answers cannot be correct.

37. a)

While nitrates are highly soluble, silver chloride is not. The precipitate is one of the products, as the reactants are both soluble (they are both in aqueous solution).

38. c)

This will make sure that all the silver nitrate has been used up.

a) may not be sufficient if the concentration of the calcium chloride solution is much lower than that of the silver nitrate. b) will help the reaction occur faster but will not determine which reactant is in excess. d) may actually have the opposite effect, if there are pockets of unmixed and therefore unreacted silver nitrate remaining.

39. b)

You can find this answer by balancing the chemical equation, converting the grams of AgCl to moles of AgCl and then corresponding number of moles of silver nitrate that must have reacted, and finally dividing this quantity by 0.05 L (50 mL) to get the molarity.

a) is the answer you would get if you found the number of moles but stopped before dividing by the volume; c) is the answer you would get if you misbalanced the chemical equation and had 2 moles of silver chloride produced for every one mole of silver nitrate reacting; d) is the answer you would get if you found the number of grams of silver chloride that reacted.

40. c)

This is an example of thermodynamic equilibrium, and shows a change in favor of increased entropy, but it does not show a colligative property in action.

a) is an example of boiling point depression, b) is an example of osmotic pressure, and d) is an example of vapor point lowering (the pure gasoline has more particles existing as a vapor than the contaminated, and so is more likely to catch fire).

41. a)

Weaker acids have a smaller Ka because they fail to dissociate as well in solution.

Since they have larger Ka's, b) and c) cannot be correct, and we know the K_a, so d) is also not right.

42. b)

Ka = [H+][F-] / [HF]

$5.6 \times 10^{-4} = x^2 / (1.5-x)$

$x^2 + 0.00056x - 0.00045 = 0$

Solve for the roots of the quadratic equation and take the positive solution, 0.021

pH = -log [H+] = - log (0.021) = 1.67

a) is the incorrect answer you would get if you stopped with the solution of the quadratic equation; c) is the answer you would get if you found the negative log of the Ka of HF, and d) is the answer you would get if you found the pKa of HF.

43. a)

The pKa is found by taking the negative log of the Ka, which gives an answer of 7.1.

d) is incorrect because the pKa is a constant and does not depend on the concentration of the solution in question.

44. c)

The sign must be changed for the iron half-reaction to account for the direction it is proceeding.

If the coefficients in the equation are wrongly taken into account to modify the value of E^0 for each half cell (that is, multiplying E^0 for the iron half-reaction by 2 and for the chlorine half-reaction by 3 in order to balance the number of electrons transferred) you will get a) as an incorrect answer, or b) if the signs are reversed in the wrong direction. d) is the incorrect answer you would find if you correctly calculated the value without using the coefficients but did change the signs in the wrong direction.

45. a)

This is shown by the positive value of the cell potential. Since we know the cell potential we do not need to know ΔS or ΔH to know whether the reaction is spontaneous.

46. c)

The equation is balanced and the same ions do not appear on both sides of the equations.

a) does not take into account that NaCl is aqueous and should be split into its component ions, and then cancel out; b) is not balanced, and d) is balanced but not broken down into ions to find what cancels

47. d)

The ideal gas law is: $PV = nRT$

At STP, P = 1 atm. We can find the temperature in Kelvin by adding 273.15, giving an answer of 308.15. If we know that methane is CH_4, we can calculate n, the number of moles, using the molar mass (16.04 g/mol) = 1.56 moles. From there, plugging into the equation, we find:

$(1) * V = (1.56) * (0.08206) * (308.15)$

$V = 39.44$ L

a) is the answer you would get if you used the number of grams, rather than mols, for n. b) is the answer you would get if you used the temperature in degrees Celsius rather than Kelvin. c) is the answer you would get if you made both of these mistakes in combination.

48. b)

This can be determined by first figuring out the number of moles of gas present based on the volume at STP, since 1 mole of a gas at STP occupies 22.4 L of volume; and then comparing that number to the mass to find the apparent molar mass.

40.0 L * (1 mol / 22.4 L) = 1.79 mol

1.79 mol * (x grams / 1 mol) = 50.1 grams – solve algebraically:

1.79x = 50.1

1.79x / 1.79 = 50.1 / 1.79

x = 28 grams, the molar mass of nitrogen gas (N_2).

The molar mass of carbon dioxide is 44.01, as is nitrous oxide; and butane's is 58.1, so answers a), c), and d) are incorrect.

49. b)

Dalton's law of partial pressures is:

$P(CO_2) = P(total) * (moles \ CO_2 / moles \ total)$

$2.1 \ g \ CO_2 * (1 \ mol / 44.01 \ g) = 0.12 \ moles$

$6.7 \ g \ N_2 * (1 \ mol / 28.02 \ g) = 0.36 \ moles$

$P(CO_2) = 0.5 \ atm \ (0.12 \ mol/0.36 \ mol) = .17 \ atm$

a) is the incorrect answer you would get if you took the ratio of masses rather than of moles; c) is what you would get if you forgot that nitrogen gas was diatomic and used a molar mass of 14.01 g instead of 28.02. d) is what you would get if you inverted the ratio of carbon dioxide to nitrogen.

50. c)

Warming the solution will actually increase the solubility of potassium chloride, which means the solution will become unsaturated rather than supersaturated (which could be achieved by carefully cooling the solution).

a) is true as gases become less soluble when the solution is warmed; b) is incorrect as ionic compounds interact preferentially with polar molecules; and d) is incorrect because the increased solubility results because of its effect to relieve the gas pressure in the system.

51. a)

$Mg(OH)_2 \leftrightarrow Mg^{2+} + 2\,OH^-$

$K_{sp} = [Mg^{2+}][OH^-]^2$

$K_{sp} = [x][2x]^2$

$K_{sp} = 2x^3$

$5.61 \times 10^{-12} = 2x^3$

Divide both sides by two and use calculator to get the cubic root, 0.000141. Thus $[Mg^{2+}]$ = 0.000141 M, and since there is a 1:1 ratio between this and the reactant, we can use this number to find the number of grams dissolved in 100 mL (0.1 L) using stoichiometric analysis:

0.000141 mol/L * (0.1L) * (58.32 g / 1 mol) = 0.00081 g

b) is the incorrect answer you would get if you failed to use the coefficient of 2 for the hydroxide. c) is the incorrect answer you would get if you failed to square the hydroxide concentration. d) is the incorrect answer you would get if you made both of these errors.

52. c)

This aligns with Bohr's model of the atom rather than the more complex electron configurations that exist in the quantum model.

a), c), and d) are all accurate descriptions of the quantum model.

53. c)

The lowest-energy 4f orbital will fill first, followed by 5d, followed by 6s.

54. c)

First, find the molarity based on the amount of acid dissolved using the molar mass of hypochlorous acid (HClO):

6 g HClO * (1 mol / 52.46 g) = 0.114

0.114 mol / 0.25 L = 0.46 M

For the reaction HClO $\longleftrightarrow$ H+ + Cl-, we can set [H+] and [Cl-] each equal to x, and [HClO] equal to 0.46 – x, and then solve the resulting quadratic equation for x to get x = 1.2 x 10^{-4}. This gives the concentration of hydrogen ions, but not hydroxide. We must use Kw to find that, using the equation:

Kw = [H+][OH-]

1.0x10-14 = (1.2 x 10^{-4}) * x

x = 8.7 x 10^{-11}

a) is the answer you would get if you only found the concentration of HClO; b) is the answer you would get if you found the concentration of hydrogen ions. d) is incorrect because Kw is a constant and does not vary with different acids.

55. a)

The negative log of the [H+].

b) is the answer you would get if you took the negative log of the [OH-], c) if you took the negative log of the Ka, and d) if you took the negative log of the [HClO].

56. d)

The formation of product would slow down as the enzyme ran out of reactant A; the initial reaction is very quick while there is plenty of reactant available to act upon.

57. d)

Assume a hypothetical initial concentration of 0.5 M; then we get a hypothetical rate of:

R = k(0.5^2), or 0.25k

If we then halve the concentration, we get:

R = k(0.25^2), or 0.0625k

0.0625k / 0.25k = 0.25 – one quarter the original rate.

58. b)

Although HCl is a strong acid, enough of a weak base will eventually neutralize it.

a) is wrong because strong acids do dissociate completely; c) is wrong because strong acids have very large dissociation constants, and d) is wrong because HCl does indeed act as a proton donor.

59. d)

By Graham's law, the rate of effusion of a gas is inversely proportional to the square root of its molar mass. Therefore the gas with the lowest molar mass will have the fastest effusion, and methane is the option with the lowest molar mass.

60. b)

This is not related to hydrogen bonding.

a) is incorrect because the unique hexagonal structure of ice is directed by hydrogen bonding between molecules; c) is wrong because the hydrogen bonding between molecules is what makes it difficult to disrupt the surface of a body of water; and d) is incorrect because the bonding requires an extra input of energy to raise the temperature to break those bonds.

Free Response Answers

1.

(a.) Describe the process of calorimetry/using a calorimeter – 1 pt

1/2 pt apiece for describing up to 2 sources of error; for example: heat loss to the surroundings or to the calorimeter itself, poor mixing of reactants

(b.) $2Mg + O_2 \rightarrow 2MgO$, or

$Mg + \frac{1}{2} O_2 \rightarrow MgO$

-1 pt for correctly writing reactants/product

-1 pt for correctly balancing

(c.) To find the ΔH:

(1 pt for showing the work for this) Find the enthalpy for the reaction:

$Mg + 2H^+ \rightarrow Mg^{2+} + H_2$

$\Delta T = 10.5$ ºC

0.2 g Mg * (1 mol Mg / 24.31 g Mg) = 0.0082 mol Mg

$q = mc\Delta T$

q = (100 g HCl) * (4.18 J/g·°C) * (10.5ºC) = 4389 J = 4.389 kJ

$\Delta H = -q = -4.389$ kJ

-4.389 kJ / 0.0082 mol Mg = -535 kJ/mol

(1 pt for showing the work for this) Find the enthalpy for the reaction:

$MgO + 2H^+ \rightarrow Mg^{2+} + H_2O$

$\Delta T = 7.4$ ºC

1 g MgO * (1 mol MgO / 40.3 g MgO) = 0.025 mol MgO

$q = mc\Delta T$

q = (100 g HCl) * (4.18 J/g·°C) * (7.4ºC) = 3093 J = 3.093 kJ

$\Delta H = -q = -3.093$ kJ

-3.093 kJ / 0.025 mol Mg = -124 kJ/mol

(1 pt for showing the work for this)

$$H_2 + 1/2O_2 \rightarrow H_2O \qquad\qquad -259\ kJ/mol$$

$$Mg + 2H^+ \rightarrow Mg^{2+} + H_2 \qquad\qquad -535\ kJ/mol$$

$$+\quad \underline{Mg^{2+} + H_2O \rightarrow MgO + 2H^+} \qquad \underline{125\ kJ/mol}$$

(1 pt for correct answer) -669 kJ/mol

(d.) Exothermic (1 pt) because of negative change in enthalpy (1 pt)

2.

(a.) Low temperature (1 pt)

Because particles at low temperatures are moving so slowly, they are more likely to interact and the intermolecular forces' effect can no longer be discounted. (1 pt).

If temperatures are low enough to deviate from ideal gas behavior, calculations of volume will be too high because they will not account for the additional intermolecular attractive forces in effect. (1 pt)

High pressure (1 pt)

Because particulars under high pressure are more likely to be forced into proximity to interact, similar to high temperature situations (1 pt).

This would also make the volume lower than accounted for by ideal gas laws. (1 pt)

(b.) (1 pt for showing the work for this) – Find the number of moles of each gas.

Let x be the number of moles of either gas.

$[(32\ g\ /\ mol) * x] + [(28\ g\ /\ mol) * x] = 20\ g$

$32x + 28x = 20$

$60x = 20$

$x = 0.33\ mol\ N_2$ and $0.33\ mol\ O_2 = 0.66\ mol$ total

(1 pt for showing the work for this) – Find the volume.

PV = nRT

V = nRT / P

V = (0.66 * 0.08206 * 350) / 1

V = 18.9 L

(1 pt for showing the work for this) – Find the density.

D = M/V

D = 20g/18.9 L

D = 1.1 g/L (1 pt for correct answer)

3.

(a.) $2\ NO + 2\ H_2 \rightarrow N_2 + 2\ H_2O$

1 pt for correctly writing reactant/products, 1 pt for correct coefficients

(b.) The general rate can be written as: rate = $k[NO]^x[H_2]^y$

Comparing the rates between reactions with different concentrations of hydrogen gas, we can set up the following to find the value for y: Rate 1 / Rate 3 = $k[NO]^x[H_2]^y / k[NO]^x[H_2]^y$

Canceling out the $k[NO]^x$ from the top and bottom of the expression, we get:

$(0.004/0.0080) = [H_2]^y$

And substituting the concentration gives:

$(0.004/0.0080) = (0.050)^y/(0.10)^y$

$0.5 = (0.05/0.1)^y$

$0.5 = (0.5)^y$

Therefore y = 1 (1 pt for correct answer, 1 for setting up correctly and showing work)

Once y is known we can use it to find x.

Rate 1 / Rate 2 = $k[NO]^x[H_2]^y / k[NO]^x[H_2]^y$

$(0.0120 / 0.004) = k(0.05^x)(.05^1) / k(0.1^x)(0.15)^1$

The constants again cancel.

$3 = (.05^x)(.05) / (.1^x)(.15)$

$3 = (.05^x)/(.1^x) * (.05/.15)$

$3 = (.05/.1)^x * (.33)$

$3 = (.5^x) * .33$

$9 = .5^x$

$\log 9 = x \log .5$

$0.95 = x * -.301$

$x = 3.1 \approx 3$ (1 pt for correct answer, 1 for setting up correctly and showing work)

To find k, choose any of the three sets of data and solve for k, including units (example uses Set 1):

$Rate = k[NO]^3[H_2]$

$k=(0.004 \text{ M/min})/(.05 \text{ M})^3(0.05 \text{ M})$

$k=(0.004 \text{ M/min})(.05)^3(.05)M^4$

$k = 640 \text{ M}^{-3}\text{min}^{-1}$

(1 pt for finding k, ½ pt if k is wrong but work is set up correctly)

Rate expression: (1 pt for correct answer)

$Rate = 6.4 \times 10^2[NO]^3[H_2]$

4.

$MgCl_2$ will have the greatest effect, because of the equation for freezing point depression:

$\Delta T = iK_f m$

The change in temperature depends on i, the van t'Hoff factor, as well as the molality. So for NaCl, i=2 because of the 2 ions it breaks into; for $MgCl_2$ i will be 3.

For NaCl: $\Delta T = (2) (1.86) (.2) = .744$

For $MgCl_2$: $\Delta T = iK_f m = (3)(1.86)(.15) = .837$; the new freezing point would be -0.837ºC.

We can discount sucrose because it will remain as one unit when dissolved, so i =1 and it has the smallest molality as well – the value for ΔT must be the smallest, then.

5.

(a.) NaCl. All of these have an effective +1 nuclear charge, but because Na's electrons are only in the 3rd energy level compared to the higher levels for the other two, the distance between the two nuclei will be the shortest and thus the bond here will be the strongest. (1 pt for answer, 1 pt for explanation)

(b.) NaBr – it will have the lowest lattice enthalpy because of the relative weakness of its bond compared to the others, making it easier to interact with the polar water molecules. (1 pt for answer, 1 pt for explanation)

6.

(a). 1 pt for each structure:

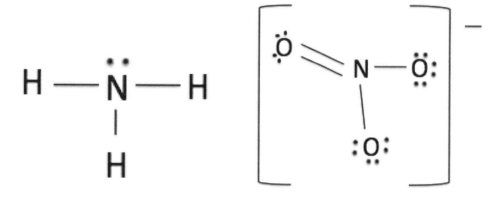

(b.) Ammonia – trigonal pyramidal; nitrate – trigonal planar. (1/2 pt for each correct answer.)

The lone pair of electrons on ammonia repels the electrons in the bonds with the hydrogen atoms, which creates the pyramidal shape, whereas the lack of lone pair in nitrate allows the planar shape, which maximizes the distances between the bonds to hydrogens. (1 pt for explanation)

7.

(a.) $2 HNO_3 + 3 H_3AsO_3(\rightarrow 2 NO + 3 H_3AsO_4 + H_2O$

(b.) (½ pt for each correct answer + ½ pt for elaboration) Possible answers include:

- add a catalyst to lower activation energy of reaction
- increase temperature to increase collisions between molecules
- increase concentration of reactants to increase collisions between molecules

Practice Examination 2

Multiple Choice Questions

1. Exactly one mole of hydrogen gas is isolated by the electrolysis of tap water. What is the mass of the sample of hydrogen?

    a) 1.00782 g, because the sample of H gas is composed of only the most common isotope of hydrogen, ^1H

    b) 1.00794 g, because the sample of H gas is composed mostly of ^1H and a small amount of the heavier isotope ^2H

    c) 3.0219 g, because hydrogen gas, H_2, is diatomic and composed of an equal mixture of the isotopes ^1H and ^2H.

    d) 2.0159 g, because hydrogen gas, H_2, is diatomic and composed mostly ^1H and a small amount of the heavier isotope ^2H

2. A sample of a nitrogen oxide is found to contain 69.6 % oxygen by mass. What is its empirical formula?

    a) NO_2

    b) N_2O_4

    c) NO

    d) N_2O

3. Which of the following electronic transitions in the hydrogen atom would emit a photon of the shortest wavelength?

    a) n=3 → n=1

    b) n=3 → n=2

    c) n=4 → n=2

    d) n=6 → n=3

4. The following are the first four ionization energies (in electron volts, eV) of different elements. Which one is most likely that of sodium?

a) 9.32, 18.21, 153.9, 217.7

b) 8.30, 25.15, 37.93, 259.4

c) 5.14, 47.2, 71.6, 98.9

d) 7.65, 15.0, 80.14, 109.2

5. Consider the following photoelectron spectrum of unknown element M:

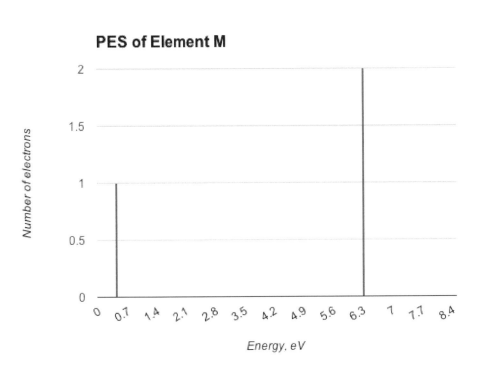

What is the formula of the chloride this element would most likely form?

a) MCl

b) MCl_2

c) MCl_4

d) This element is a noble gas, it will not form a chloride.

6. Arrange the following ions in order of increasing radius: S^{2-}, Cl^-, K^+

a) $S^{2-} < Cl^- < K^+$

b) $K^+ < Cl^- < S^{2-}$

c) $Cl^- < K^+ < S^{2-}$

d) These ions have the same electron configuration, so they will be the same size.

7. Analysis of an organic molecule provided the following mass spectrum, two double peaks at mass/charge 94 and 96, and 79 and 81, and a single peak at 15:

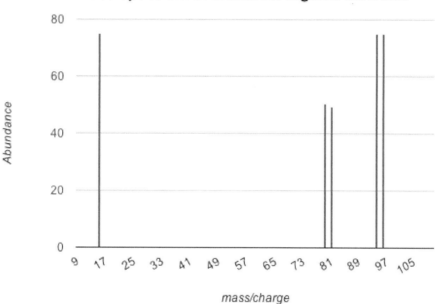

What is the most likely formula of the organic molecule?

a) CH_3Br

b) C_6H_6O

c) NH_2Br

d) CH_2Br_2

8. Which of the following bonds would be expected to have the highest bond dipole moment?

    a) O-F
    b) N-Cl
    c) C-S
    d) B-F

9. Beta-carotene ($C_{40}H_{56}$) is orange in color, while cholesterol ($C_{27}H_{46}O$) is a colorless solid. What is the best explanation for the difference between these two organic compounds?

    a) Beta-carotene is larger and contains more electrons, and larger molecules tend to be more intensely colored.

    b) Beta-carotene is difficult to purify, and contains colored impurities.

    c) More energy is required to cause the bonds of cholesterol to vibrate, compared to beta-carotene.

    d) The energy required for molecular electronic transitions is lower in beta-carotene than in cholesterol.

10. Calculate the number of moles of oxygen gas required to react with 62.0 g phosphorus (molar mass of P = 31.0 g/mol) to yield phosphorus pentoxide, according to the equation:

$$4\,P + 5\,O_2 \rightarrow 2\,P_2O_5$$

    a) 2 mol
    b) 2.5 mol
    c) 5 mol
    d) 10 mol

11. Which of the following is the correct formula for chromium (III) oxide?

a) Cr_3O

b) CrO_3

c) Cr_3O_2

d) Cr_2O_3

12. A sample of 50.0 mL of 0.250 M Ba(OH)$_2$ is titrated with 0.500 M HCl. What volume of hydrochloric acid is needed to completely neutralize the barium hydroxide?

a) 5 mL

b) 25 mL

c) 50 mL

d) 100 mL

13. Which gas might be expected to deviate the least from behavior predicted by the ideal gas law?

a) He

b) Xe

c) SO_3

d) NH_3

14. Which of the following particulate diagrams best illustrates the reaction of hydrogen gas and nitrogen gas to produce ammonia (NH₃) in a rigid container?

a)

b)

c)

d)

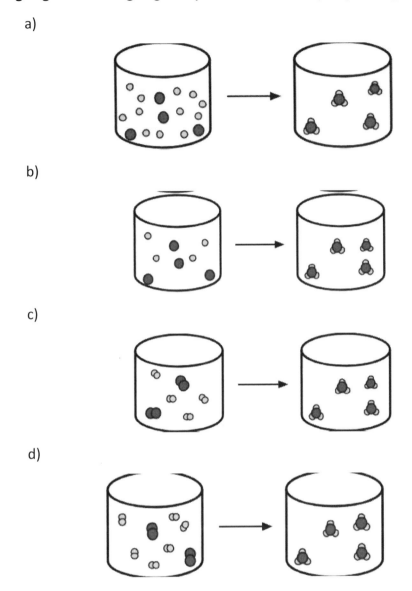

15. A sealed container contains 3.0 moles helium (4.00 g/mol), 2.0 moles neon (20.18 g/mol) and 1.0 mole argon (39.95 g/mol). The partial pressure of helium in the container is 5.0 atm. What is the total pressure in the container?

   a) atm

   b) 10.0 atm

   c) 320 atm

   d) 3840 atm

16. What is the concentration of potassium ions in a solution consisting of 1.74 g (0.0100 mol) potassium sulfate dissolved in water and diluted to a final volume of 100 mL?

   a) 0.050 mol/L

   b) 0.100 mol/L

   c) 0.200 mol/L

   d) mol/L

17. The best explanation for the very low solubility of water in hexane is:

   a) The weak solvation of H^+ and O^{2-} ions by hexane

   b) Water molecules would disrupt the very strong intermolecular H-bonds of hexane molecules.

   c) Water reacts with hexane to form hydrogen and CO_2.

   d) The weakness of the intermolecular interaction of very polar water molecules with nonpolar hexane molecules.

The next two questions refer to the following organic molecules:

a) 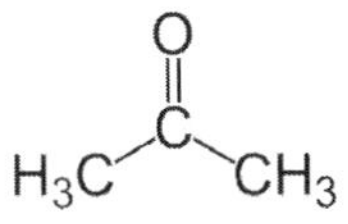 H_3C—C(=O)—CH_3

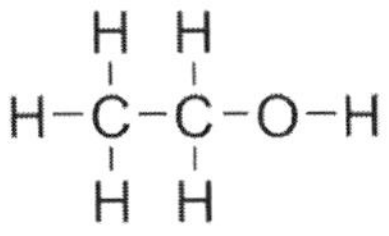

b) H–C(H)(H)–C(H)(H)–O–H

c) H_3C—C(=O)—NH_2

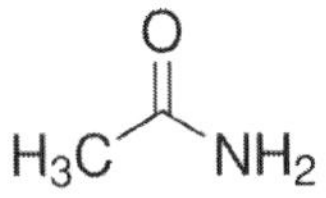

d) 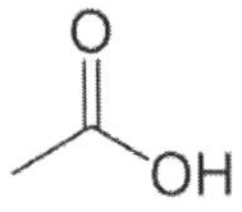 C(=O)–OH

18. Which of the above organic molecules will NOT form strong intermolecular hydrogen bonds with itself?

19. Which of the above organic molecules does NOT contain a π-bond?

20. Which of the following compounds would be expected to have the lowest boiling point?

a) Methane

b) Methanol (CH_3OH)

c) Iodomethane

d) Methylamine (CH_3NH_2)

21. Which of the following molecules does NOT have a linear geometry?

a) Hydrogen cyanide, HCN

b) Sulfur dioxide, SO_2

c) Carbon dioxide, CO_2

d) Acetylene, HCCH

22. A sample of an unknown element displays the following properties:

- **it conducts electricity as a solid**
- **it can be drawn into a wire and hammered into a thin sheet**
- **it is silver-white in color and lustrous**
- **it melts at over 2000 K**

What element is this?

a) Xenon

b) Iodine

c) Selenium

d) Platinum

23. What is the best explanation for the observation that diamond is hard and graphite is soft?

a) Diamond has a covalent structure while graphite is ionic.

b) Diamond has a 3-dimensional structure of sp^3 hybridized carbon atoms, while graphite has a 2-dimensional structure of sp^2 hybridized carbon atoms.

c) The carbon-carbon bonds in diamond are shorter and stronger than those in graphite.

d) Diamond has an ordered, crystalline structure while graphite is amorphous.

24. An aqueous solution of hydrobromic acid is to be neutralized with calcium hydroxide solution.   Which beaker, A, B, C, or D, contains just enough calcium hydroxide to neutralize the hydrobromic acid?

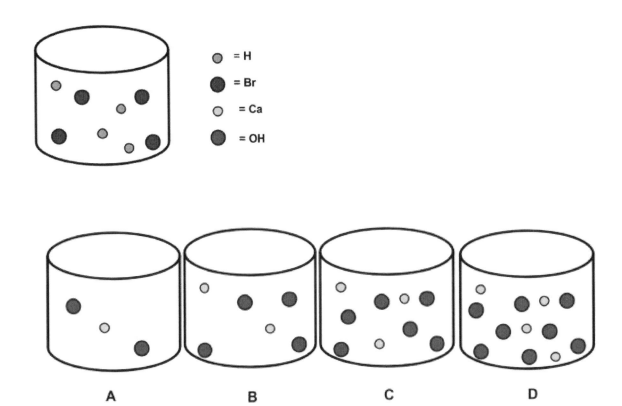

25. Consider the reaction below in a rigid iron vessel, starting with 1.00 atm nitrogen and 3.00 atm hydrogen, total pressure 4.00 atm. Assuming a constant temperature and ideal behavior, what will be the final total pressure in the vessel if the reaction goes to completion?

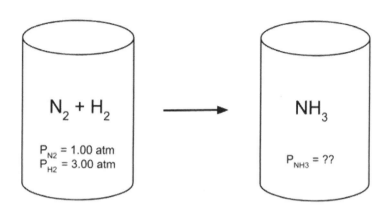

a) atm

b) 2.0 atm

c) atm

d) 4.0 atm

26. What is the excess reagent, and how many moles of excess reactant remain when 120.0 mL of 1.0M hydrochloric acid reacts with 60.0 mL of 0.75M barium hydroxide?

a) HCl, 0.030 mol excess

b) HCl, 0.060 mol excess

c) $Ba(OH)_2$, 0.030 mol excess

d) $Ba(OH)_2$, 0.060 mol excess

27. Consider the following unbalanced redox reaction between permanganate and iodide:

$$H^+ + MnO_4^- + I^- \rightarrow I_2 + Mn^{2+} + H_2O$$

When the equation is balanced, what is the coefficient for the iodine produced by the reaction?

a) 1
b) 3
c) 4
d) 5

28. Consider the following reaction coordinate diagram for the reaction A + 2B → 3C + D:

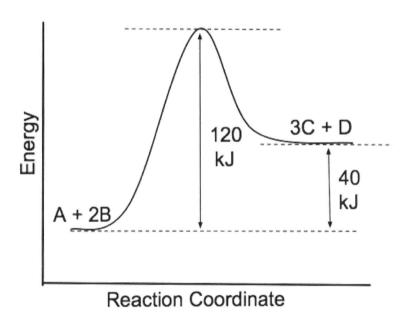

What would the energy change be if 2 moles of A reacted?

a) + 40 kJ

b) + 80 kJ

c) + 160 kJ

d) + 240 kJ

29. Arrange these four metals by increasing ease of oxidation, given the following data:

$$Zn^{++} + 2e^- \rightleftarrows Zn \ (E^o = -0.763 \ V)$$

$$Fe^{++} + 2e^- \rightleftarrows Fe \ (E^o = -0.409 \ V)$$

$$Ni^{++} + 2e^- \rightleftarrows Ni \ (E^o = -0.23 \ V)$$

$$Cu^+ + e^- \rightleftarrows Cu \ (E^o = +0.522 \ V)$$

a) Zn<Fe<Ni<Cu

b) Zn<Cu<Fe<Ni

c) Ni<Fe<Zn<Cu

d) Cu<Ni<Fe<Zn

30. Consider a galvanic cell: $Zn \mid Zn^{++} \parallel Ag^+ \mid Ag$, with the following half-cell reduction potentials:

$$Zn^{++} + 2e^- \rightleftarrows Zn \ (E^o = -0.763)$$

$$Ag^+ + e^- \rightleftarrows Ag \ (E^o = +0.800)$$

What is the balanced equation and the standard electrical potential of the cell?

a) $Zn^{++} + 2Ag \rightarrow 2Ag^+ + Zn \ (E^o = +0.037 \ V)$

b) $Zn + 2Ag^+ \rightarrow Zn^{++} + 2Ag \ (E^o = +1.56 \ V)$

c) $Zn + 2Ag^+ \rightarrow Zn^{++} + 2Ag \ (E^o = +2.36 \ V)$

d) $Zn + 2Ag^+ \rightarrow Zn^{++} + 2Ag \ (E^o = -0.037 \ V)$

31. In an electroplating experiment with an Au^{3+} solution, how much gold is plated if 10.0 amps are applied for 300 seconds?

a) 0.010 mol

b) 0.10 mol

c) mol

d) 10.0 mol

32. A reaction, A → 2B, is monitored at constant temperature in a closed vessel. How much A and B will be present after 60 seconds?

Time (seconds)	A (mol)	B (mol)
0	10.0	0
15	7.5	5.0
30	5.6	8.8

a) mol A, 10 mol B

b) 4.2 mol A, 11.6 mol B

c) mol A, 13.7 mol B

d) 2.3 mol A, 15.4 mol B

33. The initial rate of a reaction, A + B → C, is measured at various concentrations.

Initial [A]	Initial [B]	Initial Rate (mmol/sec)
0.20 M	0.25 M	5.0
0.40 M	0.25 M	20
0.40 M	0.50 M	20

What is the rate law for the reaction?

a) k[A]

b) k[A]^2

c) k[A][B]

d) k

34. Consider the following reaction coordinate diagram for the reaction A + B → C

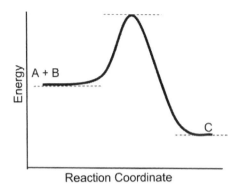

If a catalyst is added to the reaction, which new reaction coordinate diagram below will best represent the reaction? The new energy curves are colored; the original curve is dotted. Green arrows indicate changes in energy.

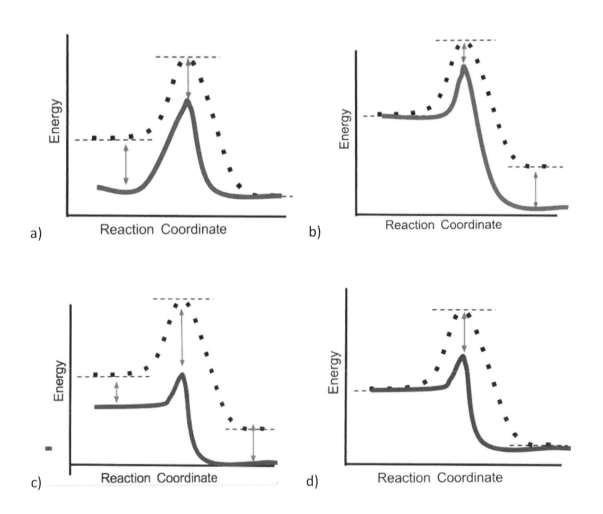

35. Two reactions are illustrated by reaction coordinate diagrams below.

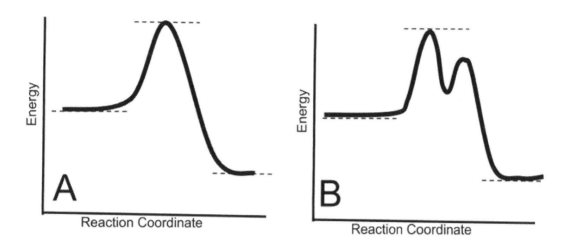

Which of the following statements is true?

a) Reaction **A** is exothermic, while reaction **B** is endothermic.

b) Reaction **B** has two energy maxima, and will occur at a slower rate than **A**.

c) The rate of reaction **A** can be increased by a catalyst, while the rate of **B** cannot.

d) Reaction **A** does not involve the formation of a short-lived intermediate, while reaction **B** does.

36. Which of the following transformations is most likely to benefit from the addition of a catalyst?

a) The reaction of hydrogen and nitrogen to give ammonia

b) The sublimation of dry ice (solid CO_2) at room temperature.

c) The reaction of $Ag^=$ and Cl^- ions to form solid AgCl in solution

d) The reaction of acetic acid with sodium hydroxide to give sodium acetate.

37. The Maxwell-Boltzmann distribution curve of a reactant gas at two temperatures is shown below.

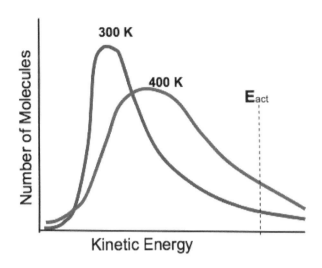

Which of the following is an accurate interpretation of this diagram?

a) The reaction proceeds more rapidly at 300 K because high point in the curve is higher.

b) The reaction proceeds more rapidly at 400 K because the high point in the curve is lower

c) The reaction proceeds more rapidly at 300K because there are fewer gas molecules at 400 K than at 300 K

d) The reaction proceeds more rapidly at 400K because the number of molecules above the activation energy E_{act} is greater than at 300K.

38. Consider the following samples of hydrocarbon gases, in sealed containers, each at 25 °C:

Gas	Ethane	Propane	Butane
Formula	C_2H_6	C_3H_8	C_4H_{10}
Molar Mass (g/mol)	30	44	58
Pressure (atm)	2.0	3.0	0.5

Assuming ideal behavior, which sample has the highest average kinetic energy per molecule?

a) Ethane

b) Propane

c) Butane

d) Each sample has the same average kinetic energy per molecule.

39. Considering the gases in question 8 above, which sample will have the highest mean speed per molecule?

a) Ethane

b) Propane

c) Butane

d) Each sample has the same mean speed per molecule.

40. A piece of iron (50 g, specific heat = 0.45 J/g·°C) was heated to 100°C then placed in a beaker of water (250 mL, specific heat = 4.18 J/g·°C) at 20°C and the temperature was allowed to equilibrate. Which of the following is the best description of the final temperature of the system?

a) The temperature will be closer to 100 °C than 20 °C

b) The temperature will be closer to 20 °C than 100 °C

c) The temperature will be 60 °C, exactly halfway between 20 °C and 100 °C

d) There is not enough information provided to determine the final temperature.

41. A gas sample is heated, so that the average kinetic energy of the particles in a sample doubles. Which of the following would describe the temperature change that occurred in the system?

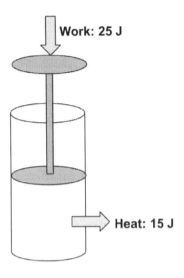

a) 200 K to 400 K
b) 50°C to 100°C
c) 0 K to 100 K
d) 0°C to 100°C

42. The piston below is compressed and radiates some heat to the environment. What is the net energy change inside the piston?

a) -40 J
b) -15 J
c) +10 J
d) +40 J

43. How much energy would it take to heat 100 g of ice at − 10°C to water at + 20 °C?
Use the following heat capacities: Specific heat of ice = 2.09 J/g·°C, heat of fusion of
water = 334 J/g, specific heat of water = 4.18 J/g·°C, heat of vaporization of water =
2257 J/g.

    a) 4390 J
    b) 10.5 kJ
    c) 43.9 kJ
    d) 269.2 kJ

44. A 190 g piece of copper absorbs 1600 J of heat and increases in temperature from
10°C to 35°C. Determine the specific heat of the copper sample.

    a) 0.20 J/g·°C
    b) 0.34 J/g·°C
    c) 0.50 J/g·°C
    d) 0.75 J/g·°C

45. Given the following data, which carbon-oxygen compound would be expected to
have the strongest carbon-oxygen bond?

Compound	C-O bond length, Å	C-O bond order
Methanol, CH_3OH	1.43	1
Sodium carbonate, Na_2CO_3	1.30	1.33
Carbon dioxide, CO_2	1.16	2
Carbon monoxide, CO	1.13	~3

    a) methanol
    b) sodium carbonate
    c) carbon monoxide
    d) carbon dioxide

46. The following diagrams represent a substance in three different states:

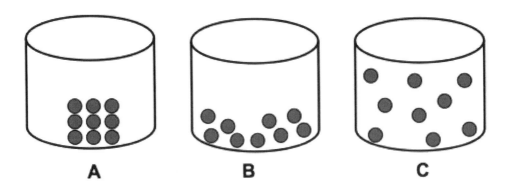

A   B   C

Which entry has the transformation and energy correctly labeled?

a) A→ C, Sublimation, exothermic
b) C → A, Condensation, endothermic
c) A → B, melting, exothermic
d) A → C, sublimation, endothermic

47. Which of the following transformations would have an energy change equal in magnitude but opposite in sign?

a) Melting and vaporization
b) Sublimation and vaporization
c) Condensation and vaporization
d) Condensation and sublimation

48. The enthalpy of solution of sodium hydroxide dissolved in water is -44.4 kJ/mol. 80.0 g sodium hydroxide is dissolved in 1.50 L of water at 25 °C. Assuming the specific heat of water is 4.18 J/g°C, what is the temperature change of the solution?

a) 10.8 °C
b) 23.6 °C
c) 26.4 °C
d) 39.2 °C

49. Arrange the following in terms of increasing bond enthalpy: H-H, H-F, H-Cl, H-Br, H-I, given the following:

Bond	Bond Length (pm)
H-H	74
H-F	92
H-Cl	127
H-Br	141
H-I	161

a) H-H < H-Cl < H-F < H-Br < H-I
b) H-H < H-I < H-Br < H-Cl < H-F
c) H-Cl < H-F < H-Br < H-I < H-H
d) H-I < H-Br < H-Cl < H-H < H-F

50. Based on the table of average bond energies below, calculate the change in enthalpy for the reaction (ΔH_{rxn}) between ethylene (CH_2CH_2) and Br_2 to form CH_4Br_2.

Bond	Energy (kJ)
C-C	348
C=C	614
C-H	413
C-Br	276
Br-Br	193

a) + 93 kJ
b) − 93 kJ
c) − 359 kJ
d) − 552 kJ

51. Given the following standard enthalpies of formation, calculate the standard enthalpy change of the following reaction: $Na_2CO_3 + 10\ H_2O \rightarrow Na_2CO_3\cdot10\ H_2O$

Compound	Na_2CO_3	H_2O	$Na_2CO_3\cdot10\ H_2O$
ΔH°_f (kJ/mol)	-1131	-286	-4081

   a) + 90 kJ/mol
   b) − 90 kJ/mol
   c) − 900 kJ/mol
   d) − 2664 kJ/mol

52. Decreasing the intermolecular forces between molecules of a pure substance would NOT result in which of the following changes?

   a) Decreased bond enthalpies
   b) Reduced melting and boiling points
   c) Reduced viscosity
   d) Reduced surface tension

53. Which of the following transformations most likely involves a decrease in entropy?

   a) $2\ NaHCO_{3\ (s)} \rightarrow Na_2CO_{3\ (s)} + H_2O_{\ (g)} + CO_{2\ (g)}$
   b) $NH_4NO_{3\ (s)} \rightarrow NH_4^{+}{}_{(aq)} + NO_3^{-}{}_{(aq)}$
   c) $N_{2(g)} + 3\ H_{2(g)} \rightarrow 2NH_{3(g)}$
   d) $CO_{2\ (s)} \rightarrow CO_{2\ (g)}$

54. A chemical reaction will always be spontaneous (thermodynamically favored) under which conditions?

   a) Exothermic with an increase in entropy
   b) Exothermic with a decrease in entropy
   c) Endothermic with a decrease in entropy
   d) Endothermic with an increase in entropy

55. Consider the reaction $X_{(g)} + Y_{(g)} \rightleftharpoons Z_{(g)}$, with K=10 at 25 °C

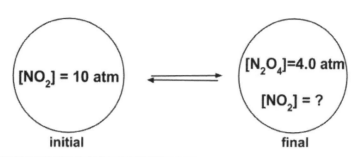

Sample	[X]	[Y]	[Z]
1	0.5	2	10
2	4	0.25	10
3	4	1	20
4	1	1	5

Which of the above samples are at equilibrium?

a) Sample 1
b) Sample 2
c) Samples 1 and 2
d) Samples 1, 2, and 4

56. Consider the reaction $2\ NO_{2(g)} \rightleftharpoons N_2O_{4\ (g)}$. A rigid container is pressurized with 10 atm NO_2, then allowed to come to equilibrium with a final concentration of 4.0 atm N_2O_4. What is K_p?

a) 1
b) 2
c) 4
d) 10

57. Given the reaction in the above question, $2\ NO_{2(g)} \rightleftarrows N_2O_{4\ (g)}$, what would the effect on the equilibrium constant K_p be of doubling the volume of the container at a constant temperature?

a) K_p will increase and favor the product, N_2O_4
b) K_p will decrease and favor the reactant, NO_2
c) The change will have no effect on the equilibrium constant.
d) It is impossible to predict the effect on the equilibrium constant

58. Given the reaction in the above question, $2\ NO_{2(g)} \rightleftarrows N_2O_{4\ (g)}$, and knowing that this reaction is exothermic and has a negative entropy, what would the effect on the equilibrium constant K_p be of increasing the temperature of the system?

a) K_p will increase and favor the product, N_2O_4
b) K_p will decrease and favor the reactant, NO_2
c) The change will have no effect on the equilibrium constant.
d) It is impossible to predict the effect on the equilibrium constant

59. 4.9×10^{-4} grams of an unknown metal hydroxide, $X(OH)_2$ will dissolve in 1000.0 mL of water. K_{sp} of the unknown metal hydroxide $= 5.8 \times 10^{-16}$.

What is the identity of the unknown metal hydroxide?

a) $Mg(OH)_2$, MW=58.3 g/mol
b) $Ni(OH)_2$, MW=92.7 g/mol
c) $Cd(OH)_2$ MW = 146.4 g/mol
d) $Pb(OH)_2$ MW=241 g/mol

60. Analyze the following titration curve. Which compound was most likely titrated to produce this curve?

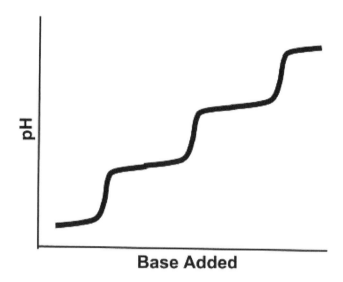

a) HBr

b) H_2SO_4

c) H_3AsO_4

d) CH_3Cl

Free Response Questions

1. Consider the following chemical reaction: $2\ NO_2Cl_{(g)} \rightarrow 2\ NO_{2(g)} + Cl_{2(g)}$

The following reaction mechanism has been proposed:

      (1) $NO_2Cl_{(g)} \rightarrow NO_{2(g)} + Cl_{(g)}$

      (2) $NO_2Cl_{(g)} + Cl_{(g)} \rightarrow NO_{2(g)} + Cl_{2(g)}$

- If the concentration of $NO_2Cl_{(g)}$ is doubled, the rate of the reaction is doubled.
- Adding $NO_{2(g)}$ to the mixture has no effect on the reaction rate.

a) Write the most plausible rate law for the above reaction.

b) Given the rate law and other information, what can be concluded about the relative reaction rates of steps (1) and (2)?

c) In the above mechanism, is $Cl_{(g)}$ a product, an intermediate, or a catalyst? Explain.

2. A buffer is prepared that is 0.10M pyridine and 0.10M pyridinium hydrochloride. The pK$_b$ of pyridine is 5.25.

    a) What is the pH of the buffer?

    b) To 100 mL of the buffer is added 1.0 mL of 2.0M HCl. What is the new pH of the buffer (neglect the small change in volume)?

    c) A pyridine/pyridinium buffer would be more useful to maintain a solution around which pH: 3, 6, or 9?

3. A 100 mL of a saturated solution of PbI$_2$ is prepared. The K$_{sp}$ is 7.0 x 10^{-9}.

    a) Write the dissociation equation for the solution.

    b) Calculate the concentration (in mol/L) of Pb^{2+} and I$^-$ in the solution.

    c) 0.020 mol KI is added to the solution. Assume it all dissolves and there is no change in volume. What is the new concentration of Pb^{2+} in the solution at equilibrium?

4. Five beakers with 0.1M aqueous solutions are placed on a benchtop. They contain:

- Ethyl alcohol
- Potassium nitrate
- Potassium carbonate
- Barium chloride
- Potassium permanganate

A series of observations and experiments are conducted. Identify which solution corresponds to the observation, and briefly explain why:

a) Which solution is strongly colored?

b) Which solution is the worst conductor of electricity?

c) Which solution is very basic?

d) Which solution will form a precipitate when a small amount of potassium chromate solution is added? What is the precipitate?

e) Which solution will react with solution (5), potassium permanganate, to produce a mixture that smells of vinegar?

5. Valproic acid, an anti-migraine medication, is a weakly acidic organic compound composed of C, H, and O. A sample of 1.02 g valproic acid was burned in excess oxygen, yielding 2.49 g CO_2 and 1.02 g H_2O.

a) Calculate the empirical formula of valproic acid?

b) Mass spectral analysis indicates that valproic acid has a mass of 144 g/mol. What is the molecular formula of valproic acid?

c) Based on the information above, which of the following is the most plausible structure for valproic acid?

6. Hydrated copper (II) sulfate, $CuSO_4 \cdot x\ H_2O$ is heated in a crucible to constant weight, generating anhydrous $CuSO_4$. The following results are obtained:

Mass of crucible	19.02 g
Mass of crucible + $CuSO_4 \cdot x\ H_2O$	28.00 g
Mass of crucible + sample after 1st heating.	25.40 g
Mass of crucible + sample after 2nd heating.	24.77 g
Mass of crucible + sample after 3rd heating.	24.76 g

a) Calculate the number of waters of hydration, x, in hydrated copper sulfate.

b) Why should the mass of the crucible + sample after the first heating, 25.40 g, not be used in the calculation? If this weight, instead of the final weight, were used, would the number of waters of hydration calculated, x, be greater or less than the correct value?

c) When drops of water are added to the anhydrous $CuSO_4$, the sample is observed to absorb the water and considerable heat is evolved. Is this process, $CuSO_4 + x\ H_2O \rightarrow CuSO_4 \cdot x\ H_2O$, endothermic or exothermic? Is the reverse reaction, $CuSO_4 \cdot x\ H_2O \rightarrow CuSO_4 + x\ H_2O$ endothermic or exothermic?

7. An iron nail weighing 0.750 g was dissolved in dilute sulfuric acid and diluted to 100.0 mL volume. A 10.0 mL aliquot of this solution was then titrated with standard 0.200M potassium permanganate solution, according to the unbalanced redox equation:

$$MnO_4^- + H^+ + Fe^{2+} \rightarrow Mn^{2+} + Fe^{3+} + H_2O$$

It took 12.08 mL of the permanganate solution to oxidize all the iron.

a) Balance the above redox equation.

b) Determine the mass of iron present in the original sample.

c) Given the result from (B), what was the purity (percent iron) of the iron nail?

d) If the nail contained a non-iron impurity that did not react with the sulfuric acid, but was oxidized by the permanganate, would the calculated purity of the nail be overestimated or underestimated?

Answer Key 2

Multiple Choice Answers

1. **(d), 2.0159 g.**

   Hydrogen is a diatomic gas (H_2), so 1 mole of hydrogen gas has 2 moles of hydrogen atoms, so (a) and (b) are not correct. Hydrogen (or any element) isolated from a natural source (like tap water) will be composed of a mixture of isotopes at their natural abundance level, in this case mostly ^1H (99.98 %, isotopic mass 1.00782 g/mol) and a very small amount of ^2H (0.02 %, isotopic mass 2.01410 g/mol), so (a) and (c) are not correct. The standard atomic mass of H is 1.00794, multiplied by 2 (hydrogen is diatomic) is 2.0159 g, which is (d).

2. **(a), NO_2**

   The sample contains 69.6 g O, and therefore (100-69.6) = 30.4 g N. That is 69.6 g / 16.0 g/mol = 4.35 mol O, and 30.4 g /14.0 g/mol = 2.17 mol N. The molar ratio of O to N is 4.35:2.17 = 2:1, so the correct empirical formula is NO_2.

   Although the sample could be N_2O_4 (or a mixture of NO_2 and N_2O_4), the empirical formula is the simplest whole number ratio of elements in a compound, so N_2O_4 can be simplified to NO_2, so (b) is not correct. (c) and (d) have different molar ratios, and therefore different mass percentages.

3. **(a), n=3 → n=1**

   The wavelength of electron transitions in the hydrogen atom can be calculated by the Rydberg formula:

   $1/\lambda = R ((1/n_1^2) - (1/n_2^2))$, where R is the Rydberg constant (1.097×10^7 m^{-1}) and n are the numbers corresponding to the energy levels, where $n_1 < n_2$.

   Application of this formula indicates that the electronic transitions between lower energy levels (e.g. n=3 → n=1) will always be higher in energy, and therefore have a shorter wavelength ($\lambda_{3-->1}$ = 97 nm), than those between higher energy levels (the other possible answers).

4. **(c), 5.14, 47.2, 71.6, 98.9**

Ionization energy is the energy required to remove an electron from an atom or ion. It doesn't take much energy to remove an electron from a partially filled orbital, but once the partially filled orbital has been emptied, it can take up to ten times more energy to remove the next electron from the lower, filled orbital. The electron configuration of sodium is $1s^2 2s^2 2p^6 3s^1$, so after the first electron is removed, the Na^+ ion has the filled, noble-gas-like $1s^2 2s^2 2p^6$ configuration, and the second ionization energy will be significantly (nearly ten times) higher. That is (c), where the first ionization energy is 5.1, and the second, is 47.2.

(a) is beryllium, $1s^2 2s^2$, with a large increase between the second and third ionization energies. (b) is boron, $1s^2 2s^2 2p^1$, with the largest increase between the third and fourth ionization energies. (d) is magnesium, $1s^2 2s^2 2p^6 3s^2$, with a large increase between the second and third ionization energies.

5. **(a), MCl**

The photoelectron spectrum shows one electron being ejected a low energy of around 0.5 eV (i.e. one electron in the element's valence shell) followed by two electrons at a much higher energy of 6.3 eV. This suggests a configuration of $1s^2 2s^1$, which is correct - this is the PES of lithium. Lithium, as an alkali metal, will lose its single electron to form an ion with a single positive charge, Li^+. Chloride, Cl^- has a single negative charge, so the compound formed by Li^+ and Cl^- will be the monochloride, LiCl or "MCl", answer (a).

6. **(b), $K^+ < Cl^- < S^{2-}$**

These three ions are isoelectronic, having the same electron configuration, $1s^2 2s^2 2p^6 3s^2 3p^6$. However, this does not mean they have the same size. They have different nuclear charges, so the K^+ electrons (nuclear charge +19) experience more positive charge than the S^{2-} electrons (nuclear charge +16), and are therefore held closer to the nucleus. This results in K^+ having a smaller ionic radius (152 pm) than Cl^- (167 pm), which in turn has a smaller radius than S^{2-} (170 pm).

7. **(a), CH₃Br**

The double peaks at mass/charge 79+81 and 94+96 suggest the presence of bromine, which exists as two isotopes of almost equal abundance, ^{79}Br and ^{81}Br. This excludes (b), which would have a molecular mass of 94 but does not contain bromine. The single peak at mass/charge 15 suggests CH_3^+. CH_3Br would contain both a Br and a CH_3, so (a) is the answer. (c), NH_2Br would show a molecular ion at 95+97 (and isn't organic), and neither it nor (d), CH_2Br_2, would show a mass peak at 15.

8. **(d), B-F**

Bonds connecting atoms of different electronegativities are polar, and the larger the difference in electronegativity the greater the dipole moment. Electronegativity increases across the periodic table, so the most electronegative element is fluorine. An element from the left of the periodic table, like boron in this case, will be much less electronegative, and will therefore have a larger bond dipole moment when bonded to F than elements closer to each other on the periodic table.

9. **(d), the energy required for molecular electronic transitions is lower in beta-carotene than in cholesterol.**

The color of a substance is determined by its absorbance of photons in the ultraviolet and visible range of the electromagnetic spectrum, which depends on the energy required for molecular electronic transitions. Most organic molecules will absorb high-energy photons in the far ultraviolet, but if the electronic transition energy becomes low enough, they will absorb lower energy photons in the visible range and appear colored.

While colored organic molecules tend to be large, molecular mass itself does not cause molecules to be colored, so (a) is not correct. Also, while some substances will rapidly become colored due to the formation of impurities (like iodomethane, which is colorless when pure but almost always appears purple due to slight decomposition), in this case the color of beta-carotene is not due to impurities, so (b) is not correct. The electromagnetic energies that cause molecules to vibrate are in the infrared, not the visible range, so (c) is not correct.

10. **(b), 2.5 mol**

First calculate the amount of phosphorus reacting: 62 g / 31 g/mol = 2 mol P

The molar ratio of oxygen to phosphorus is 5:4, so the molar amount of oxygen required is: 5/4 x 2 mol = 2.5 mol O_2

11. (d), Cr_2O_3

The numeral (III) signifies a +3 ionization state of the chromium, so Cr^{3+}. The charge on oxygen ions is O^{2-}, so 3 oxygens are required to balance the charge on two chromiums. The correct formula is Cr_2O_3

12. (c), 50 mL

First, determine the chemical equation of the titration reaction:

$Ba(OH)_2 + 2\ HCl \rightarrow BaCl_2 + 2\ H_2O$

So 2 moles of HCl are required to neutralize 1 mole of $Ba(OH)_2$

Determine the molar amount of barium hydroxide in the sample:

0.250 mol/L x 0.0500 L = 0.0125 mol $Ba(OH)_2$

The amount of HCl required to neutralize the $Ba(OH)_2$ is:

2 x 0.0125 mol = 0.0250 mol

The volume of hydrochloric acid required is:

0.0250 mol / 0.500 mol/L = 0.0500 L, which is 50 mL.

13. (a), He

The ideal gas law is based on two assumptions - that gas particles occupy no volume, and that the forces of attraction between gas molecules is zero. Since these assumptions are more likely to be incorrect for larger and more polar molecules, one would expect the small, non polar He to deviate less from ideal behavior than the much larger Xe or the larger and more polar SO_3 and NH_3. However, at high pressures and low temperatures, all gases deviate from ideality to some extent.

14. (d),

15. (b), 10.0 atm

The total pressure of an ideal gas mixture is the sum of the partial pressures of each gas, and pressure is determined by the number of moles of each gas present (it has nothing to do with molar mass). The total moles of gas in this mixture is (3.0 + 2.0 + 1.0) = 6.0 moles. The number of moles of helium is 3.0 moles, with a partial pressure of 5.0 atm, so the total pressure will be 6.0 moles/3.0 moles x 5.0 atm, or 10.0 atm.

16. (c), 0.200 mol/L

First, determine the amount of the solute, potassium sulfate, dissolved:

1.74 g / 174.3 g/mol = 0.0100 mol

There are two potassium ions per mole of potassium sulfate, K_2SO_4, so total number of moles potassium:

0.0100 mol x 2 = 0.0200 mol

The final volume is 100 mL or 0.100 L, so the concentration is:

0.0200 mol / 0.100 L = 0.200 mol / L or 200 mmol/L

17. (d), the weakness of the intermolecular interaction...

To be soluble, molecules of a solute must break intermolecular forces between themselves and form energetically favorable interactions with molecules of a solvent. Highly polar water molecules have strong intermolecular forces between themselves (dipole-dipole interactions and hydrogen bonds), and do not form strong interactions with very nonpolar hexane molecules. Therefore, (d) is correct. Water does not dissociate significantly into H^+ and O^{2-} in any solvent, so (a) is not correct. Hexane molecules are nonpolar and do not form H-bonds with themselves or solutes, so (b) is not correct. Water and hexane do not react under any normal laboratory conditions, so (c) is not correct.

18. (a), acetone

A hydrogen bond is a strong dipole-dipole interaction between a hydrogen bonded to an electronegative atom (usually N, O, or F) and a lone pair. If a molecule has no hydrogens bonded to an electronegative atom it cannot form H bonds with itself. Acetone, molecule (a), has an oxygen, but no hydrogens bonded directly to the oxygen. (b), (c), and (d) all have hydrogens directly bonded to O or N molecules and can therefore form H bonds.

19. (b), ethanol

☐-bonds are double bonds. Ethanol, (b), has only single bonds while the other three molecules have carbon-oxygen double bonds.

20. (a), methane

Boiling point is determined by the strength of the intermolecular forces between molecules. Methane is a small, nonpolar molecule that has only weak London dispersion forces as its intermolecular forces. It therefore has a very low boiling point (- 161 $^\circ$ C). Iodomethane, (c) is also relatively nonpolar but it is much larger and more polarizable, and therefore has much stronger London dispersion forces and a corresponding higher boiling point (43 $^\circ$ C). Methanol and methylamine both have highly polar O-H and N-H bonds, respectively, and can therefore form intermolecular hydrogen bonds. These result in much stronger intermolecular forces, and therefore higher boiling points (65 $^\circ$ C for methanol, - 6 $^\circ$ C for methylamine).

21. (b), Sulfur dioxide, SO_2

According to VSEPR theory, molecules are linear if the central atom(s) are bonded to two other atoms and have no lone pairs. By examining the Lewis structures of the molecules in question, we see this is the case for (a) HCN (C bonded to H and N, no lone pairs), (c) CO_2 (C bonded to two O, no lone pairs) and (d) acetylene (each C bonded to the H and the other C, no lone pairs). In SO_2, however, the S is bonded to two oxygens and has a lone pair. SO_2 has a bent geometry.

22. (d), Platinum

The properties listed are all associated with metals and metallic bonding - conductivity, malleability, ductility, lustre, and high melting point. The only metal in the list is platinum, all the other elements are nonmetals.

23. (b), Diamond has a 3-dimensional structure...

Diamond and graphite are both network covalent allotropes of carbon - they are not ionic or amorphous, so (a) and (d) are not correct. The carbon-carbon bonds in graphite are actually shorter than those in diamond, so (c) is not correct. Because it is composed of 2-dimensional sheets of sp^2 hybridized carbon atoms, layers of graphite can slide over each other relatively easily and graphite is therefore relatively soft.

24. (b),

The acid beaker shown has four orange H^+ ions. Four dark blue OH^- ions are required to neutralize them. Beaker (B) has four dark blue OH^- ions.

25. (b), 2.0 atm

The balanced chemical reaction is:

$$N_{2(g)} + 3\ H_{2(g)} \rightarrow 2\ NH_{3(g)}$$

There are 4 gas molecules on the left of the equation and 2 on the right. From the ratio of partial pressures we can deduce that there are 3 moles of H_2 for every one mole of N_2 in the container, so neither H_2 nor N_2 will be limiting; all will be consumed and converted to ammonia. The total pressure will be the total pressure of ammonia - which will be 2/4 x 4 atm, or 2.0 atm.

26. (a), HCl, 0.030 mol excess

First, determine the balanced chemical reaction:

$$Ba(OH)_2 + 2\ HCl \rightarrow BaCl_2 + 2\ H_2O$$

Now calculate the amount of each reagent added, and determine the limiting reagent :

HCl : 0.120 L x 1.0 mol/L = 0.120 mol, would produce 0.060 mol $BaCl_2$

$Ba(OH)_2$: 0.060 L x 0.75 mol/L = 0.045 mol, would produce 0.045 mol $BaCl_2$

$Ba(OH)_2$ is the limiting reagent, so HCl is the excess reagent.

It would take 0.045 mol x 2 or 0.090 moles HCl to neutralize all the $Ba(OH)_2$, so the excess HCl is:

0.120 mol - 0.090 mol = 0.030 mol

27. (d), 5

First, consider the reduction half-reaction:

$$MnO_4^- \rightarrow Mn^{2+}$$

Balance it for oxygens:

$$MnO_4^- \rightarrow Mn^{2+} + 4H_2O$$

Now balance for hydrogens:

$$8H^+ + MnO_4^- \rightarrow Mn^{2+} + 4H_2O$$

Add electrons to balance charges on both sides:

$$5e^- + 8H^+ + MnO_4^- \rightarrow Mn^{2+} + 4H_2O$$

Now consider the oxidation half reaction:

$$I^- \rightarrow I_2$$

Balance the atoms, and add electrons to balance charges:

$$2I^- \rightarrow I_2 + 2e^-$$

Reduction half-reaction has 5 e⁻ on left, oxidation has 2 e⁻ on right. Multiply reduction by 2, oxidation by 5:

$$10e^- + 16H^+ + 2MnO_4^- \rightarrow 2Mn^{2+} + 8H_2O$$

$$10I^- \rightarrow 5I_2 + 10e^-$$

And add, and cancel electrons:

$$\cancel{10e^-} + 16H^+ + 2MnO_4^- + 10I^- \rightarrow 5I_2 + 2Mn^{2+} + 8H_2O \; \cancel{+ 10e^-}$$

The balanced reaction is $16H^+ + 2MnO_4^- + 10I^- \rightarrow 5I_2 + 2Mn^{2+} + 8H_2O$, and the coefficient of iodine is 5.

28. (b), + 80 kJ

The diagram shows the energy change for 1 mole of A (40 kJ). Two moles of A will release twice this amount of energy, or 80 kJ. 120 kJ is the activation energy, and does not contribute to the final energy change of the system.

29. (d), Cu<Ni<Fe<Zn

The numbers provided are the reduction potentials, the energy of the reduction of the metal ions. Oxidation is the opposite, so the metal with the lowest reduction potential (Zn) will be the most easily oxidized.

30. (b), Zn + 2Ag$^+$ → Zn^{++} + 2Ag (E^o = + 1.56 V)

The half-cell with the lower reduction potential is flipped and its voltage inverted, so...

Zn^{++} + 2e$^-$ ⇄ Zn (E^o = - 0.763 V) becomes Zn ⇄ Zn^{++} + 2e$^-$ (E^o = + 0.763 V)

Two electrons are needed to balance the Zn half equation, so the Ag$^+$ equation is doubled.

2Ag$^+$ + 2e$^-$ ⇄ 2Ag (E^o = +0.800 V)

Note that the voltage is NOT doubled, it is an intrinsic property of substance.

The sum of the two half-reactions is Zn + 2Ag$^+$ → Zn^{++} + 2Ag (E^o = + 1.56 V).

31. (a), 0.010 mol

To determine the number of coulombs transferred, multiply amps by seconds:

10 s x 300 amps = 3000 C

Divide by Faraday's constant:

3000 C/(96500 C/mol) = 0.031 mol

Since 3 electrons would be necessary to reduce one Au^{3+} ion, the amount of gold plated would be:

0.031 mol / 3 = 0.010 mol

32. (c), 3.2 mol A, 13.7 mol B

From the data, every 15 seconds, the amount of A present decreases by 25 % (this is a first order reaction in A). So the amount of A present will be:

10 x 0.75^t, where t is the number of 15–second intervals elapsed.

And from the stoichiometry, the amount of B present will be 2 x (amount of A consumed).

Therefore, after 60 seconds:

A = 10 x 0.75^4 = 3.16 mol

B = 2 x (10-3.16) = 13.7 mol

33. (b), k[A]^2

The first two lines indicate that as [A] doubles, the rate quadruples. That means the rate Is proportional to [A]^2. The third line shows that as [B] doubles, there is no change in the rate. So [B] does not participate in the reaction. The rate law must therefore be k[A]^2.

34. (d),

A catalyst decreases only the energy of the transition state of a reaction, thereby reducing the activation energy and increasing the rate of the reaction. It does not change the energy of the reactants or products. In the above graphics, (a) reduces the energy of the reactants and transition state, (b) reduces the energy of the transition state and the product, (c) reduces the energy of the reactants, transition state and product. Only (d) reduces only the energy of the transition state.

35. (d),

Reaction **A** does not involve the formation of a short-lived intermediate, while reaction **B** does. Both **A** and **B** are exothermic, so (a) is not correct. The activation energy of **A** and **B** are identical, and the use of a catalyst in **A** and **B.**

36. (a), the reaction of hydrogen and nitrogen to give ammonia.

The reaction of hydrogen and nitrogen to give ammonia is extremely slow at room temperature, and therefore is generally conducted at high temperatures with a catalyst in a process called the Haber process. The sublimation of CO_2 (a physical, not a chemical change), precipitation of AgCl, and the reaction of acetic acid with base are all very rapid at standard conditions and normally have no need of a catalyst.

37. (d),

A Maxwell-Boltzmann diagram shows the distribution of particles by kinetic energy. For a reaction to occur, particles must have a kinetic energy above the activation energy of the reaction E_{act}, so the larger the number of particles above E_{act}, the faster the reaction. The high point on the curve itself does not matter, so (a) and (b) are not correct. There are the same number of particles in the system, just with a greater energy distribution, so (c) is not correct.

38. (d), each sample has the same average kinetic energy per molecule.

In a gas, the average kinetic energy per molecule is a function of the absolute temperature. Since these gases are at the same temperature, 25 °C, they have the same average kinetic energy.

39. (a), ethane.

Mean molecular speed is inversely proportional to molar mass at a given kinetic energy, so the molecule with the lowest molar mass will have the highest mean speed. That is ethane, (a).

40. (b), the temperature will be closer to 20 °C than 100 °C

The total amount of energy in the system will be constant, and can be estimated from the heat capacities. The iron contains about 0.5 J for each gram and degree, so 0.5 x 50 x 80 °C over the water temp = about 2000 J 'excess' heat. The energy required to heat the water is about 4 J per gram and degree, and there are 250 g (1 mL=1g) water, so 4 x 250 g = 1000 J per degree. So there is only enough 'excess' energy in the iron to heat the water sample by about 2 degrees. The final system temperature will be much closer to 20 °C than 100 °C.

41. (a), 200 K to 400 K

Particle kinetic energy depends on absolute temperature, which is measured on the Kelvin scale. The final temperature has to be twice the initial temperature in Kelvin, that is answer (a), 400/200 = 2.

42. (c), +10 J

The total amount of energy in the piston is the sum of the work and heat. 25 J are added and 15 J are lost. Because a net amount of energy is absorbed, the sign of the energy change is positive, so the answer is + 10 J.

43. (c), 43.9 kJ

Change in temperature of ice is $-10^{\circ}C$ to $0^{\circ}C$, or $10^{\circ}C$, so:

100 g x $10^{\circ}C$ x 2.09 = 2090 J

Melting of ice:

100 g x 334 J/g = 33400 J

Heating of water from $0^{\circ}C$ to $20^{\circ}C$:

100 g x 20 $^{\circ}C$ x 4.18 = 8360 J

Total = 2090 + 33400 + 8360 = 43850 J or 43.9 kJ

Note that the heat of vaporization is not used in this calculation.

44. (b), 0.34 J/g$^{\cdot \circ}$C

The temperature change is (35-10) = $25^{\circ}C$

Joules per degree is:

1600 J/25 $^{\circ}C$ = 64 J/$^{\circ}C$

The mass is 190 g, so the specific heat is

64 J/$^{\circ}C$ / 190 g = 0.34 J/g$^{\cdot \circ}$C, which is (b).

45. (c), carbon monoxide

In similar elements, shorter bonds, with higher bond orders, are stronger. Carbon monoxide, with its very short C-O bond has one of the strongest bonds known, with a bond dissociation energy of around 1072 kJ/mol.

46. (d), A → C, sublimation, endothermic

A to C is a phase change from solid to gas. This is sublimation, which requires energy, therefore it is endothermic, so (a) is not correct. C to A (b) is gas to solid (sublimation or deposition), and is exothermic. A to B (c) is solid to liquid, melting, which is endothermic.

47. (c), condensation and vaporization

Two processes will have equal and opposite energy changes if they are opposing changes in state, such as ice melting to give water and water freezing to give ice. (c), condensation and vaporization, are opposing changes in state so they will have equal and opposite energy changes. All the other pairs are not opposing changes in state but different, unrelated changes in state.

48. (d), 39.2 °C

First, calculate the amount of sodium hydroxide:

80.0 g / 40.0 g/mol = 2.00 mol NaOH

The total energy released:

2.00 mol x -44.4 kJ/mol = - 88.8 kJ

There are (1.50 L x 1 g/mL x 1000 mL/L) = 1500 g of water, so the energy per gram of water is:

- 88.8 kJ / 1500 g = 0.0592 kJ/g = or - 59.2 J/g

The energy released per gram of water is - 59.2 J (negative means energy added to the system), and it takes 4.18 J to increase 1 g by 1 °C, so:

59.2 J / 4.18 J/g·°C = 14.2 °C

So the final temperature will be:

25.0 + 14.2 °C = 39.2 °C

49. (d), H-I < H-Br < H-Cl < H-H < H-F

Bond enthalpy is the energy required to break a bond. Generally speaking, the shorter the bond length, the stronger the bond, and the greater the bond enthalpy. H-H bonds are quite strong, and would not be the weakest bond in the series, so (a) and (b) are not correct. (c) has the very long bond H-Br and H-I above H-Cl and H-F, so it is not correct. By elimination, (d) is correct.

50. (b), – 93 kJ

The change in enthalpy for a reaction is based on the enthalpy of bonds broken minus the enthalpy of bonds formed:

$\Delta H_{rxn} = \sum \Delta H_{(bonds\ broken)} - \sum \Delta H_{(bonds\ formed)}$

ΔH_{rxn} = [4(C-H) + 1(C=C) + 1(Br-Br)] - [1(C-C) + 2(C-Br) + 4(C-H)]

= [4 x 413 + 614 + 193] – [348 + 2 x 276 + 4 x 413]

= [~~4 x 413~~ + 614 + 193] – [348 + 2 x 276 + ~~4 x 413~~]

= 807 – 900

= – 93 kJ

51. (b), - 90 kJ/mol

Enthalpy change: ΔH°_f(products) - ΔH°_f(reactants)

$= -4081 - (-1131 + 10(-286))$

$= -4081 - (-3991)$

$= -90$ kJ/mol

52. (a), decreased bond enthalpies.

Melting and boiling points, viscosity, and surface tension all depend on the strength of intermolecular forces in molecules, so they would all be reduced if the intermolecular forces were decreased. Bond enthalpies have nothing to do with intermolecular forces, so they would not decrease.

53. (c), $N_{2(g)} + 3 H_{2(g)} \rightarrow 2NH_{3(g)}$

The reaction of nitrogen gas with hydrogen gas to produce ammonia involves four gas molecules reacting to form two gas molecules. This decreases the number of particles in the system, which decreases the entropy. The other transformations all involve more gas or dissolved particles in the products than in the reactants, which would result in an increase in entropy.

54. (a), Exothermic with an increase in entropy

Thermodynamic favorability of a chemical reaction is determined by the Gibbs free energy,

$$\Delta G = \Delta H - T\Delta S$$

If $\Delta G < 0$, the reaction is spontaneous.

Therefore, if ΔH is negative (reaction is exothermic) and ΔS is positive (increase in entropy) then ΔG must always be negative.

55. (c), Samples 1 and 2

The equilibrium constant is determined by K=[Z]/[X][Y]. If [Z]/[X][Y] = 10, the sample is at equilibrium. In both samples 1 and 2, [Z]/[X][Y] is 10, so they are both at equilibrium. In samples 3 and 4, [Z]/[X][Y] is 5, and the samples are not at equilibrium.

56. (a), 1

The problem can be solved as follows:

Two equivalents NO_2 are used to form 1 equivalent N_2O_4, so at 4.0 atm N_2O_4 the amount of NO_2 remaining will be (10 – 2 x 4.0) or 2.0 atm.

Compound	NO_2	N_2O_4
Initial pressure (atm)	10	0
Final Pressure (atm)	2.0	4.0

So the equation for K is

K_p = [N_2O_4] / [NO_2]^2 4.0 / (2.0)^2 = 4.0 / 4.0 = 1.0

57. (b), K_p will decrease and favor the reactant, NO_2

By Le Chatelier's principle, if you decrease the pressure on a gaseous mixture at equilibrium, the equilibrium will shift towards the side with more gas particles, in this case, toward the reactant NO_2.

58. (b), K_p will decrease and favor the reactant, NO_2

Again, by Le Chatelier's principle, increasing the temperature of an exothermic reaction, and a reaction with a negative entropy, will both tend to shift the equilibrium towards the reactants.

59. (b), Ni

If n moles of the hydroxide dissolve in water, there will be n moles of X^{2+} and 2n moles of OH^-

So, $K_{sp} = [X][OH^-]^2 = n \cdot (2n)^2 = 4n^3$

$4n^3 = 5.8 \times 10^{-16}$

$n^3 = 1.5 \times 10^{-16}$

$n = 5.3 \times 10^{-6}$

So the number of moles of the dissolved hydroxide is 5.3×10^{-6} mol.

The mass of dissolved hydroxide is given as 4.9×10^{-4} g, so the molar mass is

4.9×10^{-4} g / 5.3×10^{-6} mol = 88 g/mol, which is closest in mass to (b), Ni.

60. (c), H_3AsO_4

Each inflection point on the graph corresponds to the removal of a proton with a different pK. There are 3 inflection points, so the substance must be a triprotic acid. (c), arsenic acid, is the only triprotic acid present. Methyl chloride, (d), has no acidic hydrogens and would not produce a titration curve like this.

Free Response Answers

1.

a) The reaction is first order in NO_2Cl, and unaffected by NO_2, so the rate law is $k[NO_2Cl]$

b) Only the reactant in the first step participates in the rate law, so step (1) must be the slow, rate-limiting step. Step (2) must have a faster reaction rate than step (1).

c) $Cl_{(g)}$ is an intermediate, a short-lived species that is formed by an elementary step in a reaction then consumed in a following step, but not present in the overall reaction equation. A product is a species that is present on the right of an overall reaction equation. A catalyst is a species that increases the reaction rate, but is not consumed by the reaction. Cl is consumed by this reaction and none will be present when the reaction is complete, so it is not a catalyst.

2.

(a) First, find the pK_a: $pK_a = 14 - pK_b = 14\text{-}5.25 = 8.75$

$pH = pK_a + \log([base]/[acid]) = 8.75 + \log([0.10]/[0.10]) = 8.75 + 0.0 = 8.75$

So the pH of the buffer is 8.75

(b) 1.0 mL of 2.0M HCl is 0.0020 mol HCl

In 100 mL (0.100 L) of the buffer, there is (0.10 mol/L) x (0.10 L) = 0.010 mol pyridine. There is the same amount of pyridinium.

All the pyridine will react with the strong acid to form pyridinium, so the new amount of pyridine and pyridinium will be:

0.010 mol – 0.0020 mol = 0.008 mol pyridine, which in 100 mL corresponds to 0.08M pyridine.

0.010 mol + 0.0020 mol = 0.012 mol pyridinium, which in 100 mL corresponds to 0.12M pyridinium.

The new pH will be: $pH = pK_a + \log([base]/[acid]) = 8.75 + \log([0.08]/[0.12])$

which is $8.75 + \log (0.66) = 8.75 - 0.18 = 8.57$

(c) Buffers are most useful at maintaining pH close to their pK_as. So in the case of a pyridine buffer (pKa = 8.75) this would be around a pH of 9.

3.

(a) The solution equilibrium equation is $PbI_2 \rightleftarrows Pb^{2+} + 2I^-$

(b) Therefore, $K_{sp} = 7.0 \times 10^{-9} = [Pb^{2+}][I^-]^2$

The molar concentration of Pb^{2+}, x, will be given by $= 7.0 \times 10^{-9} = [x][2x]^2 = 4x^3$

Solving for x:

$x^3 = (7.0/4) \times 10^{-9} = 1.8 \times 10^{-9}$

$x = (1.8 \times 10^{-9})^{1/3} = 0.0012$

The concentration of Pb^{2+} is 0.0012 mol/L, and the concentration of I^- is 0.0024 mol/L

(c) 0.020 mol KI in 100 mL of solution is 0.20 mol/L KI solution. This is much higher than the initial concentration of I^- (0.0024 mol/L) so just use 0.20 mol/L as the new I^- concentration.

$K_{sp} = 7.0 \times 10^{-9} = [Pb^{2+}][I^-]^2$

So: $7.0 \times 10^{-9} = [Pb^{2+}][0.20]^2 = [Pb^{2+}][0.040]$

$[Pb^{2+}] = 7.0 \times 10^{-9}/0.040 = 1.8 \times 10^{-7}$ mol/L

4.

a) Potassium permanganate, 5. MnO_4^- is the only colored ion in the list, all other solutions would be colorless.

b) Ethyl alcohol, 1. It is a solution of a non-ionic, organic compound, and will not conduct electricity as well as the other four ionic solutions.

c) Potassium carbonate, 3. Carbonate ion is very basic, all the other substances listed are nearly neutral.

d) Barium chloride, 4. Will form the insoluble salt barium chromate, $BaCrO_4$.

e) Ethyl alcohol, 1, will react with potassium permanganate to produce acetic acid (vinegar). Potassium permanganate is a strong oxidizing agent and will oxidize the ethanol to acetic acid.

5.

(a): First, determine how many moles of CO_2 and H_2O were generated, and how much C and H this corresponds to:

moles CO_2 = 2.49 g/44.002 g/mol = 0.0566 mol, each molecule came from 1 C atom, so 0.0566 mol C

moles H_2O = 1.02 g/18.02 g/mol = 0.0566 mol, each molecule came from 2 H atoms, so 0.113 mol H

Calculate the mass percent of each element:

0.0566 mol C * 12.01 g/mol = 0.680 g C / 1.02 g compound = 66.6 % C

0.113 mol H * 1.01 g/mol = 0.114 g H / 1.02 g compound = 11.2 % H

Since this does not add up to 100 %, the remainder must be oxygen, (100 - 66.6 - 11.2) = 22.2 % O, which is 22.2% * 1.02 g / 16.0 g/mol = 0.0142 mol O

The composition of valproic acid is therefore $C_{0.0566}H_{0.113}O_{0.0142}$, which (dividing each subscript by 0.0142, and rounding to nearest number) works out to the empirical formula C_4H_8O.

(b) The mass of C_4H_8O is (12.01 x 4 + 1.01 * 8 + 16.00) = 72.1 g/mol. Valproic acid has a molar mass of 144 g/mol, which is (144/72) or two times the empirical formula, C_4H_8O x 2, or $C_8H_{16}O_2$

The correct structure for valproic acid is below:

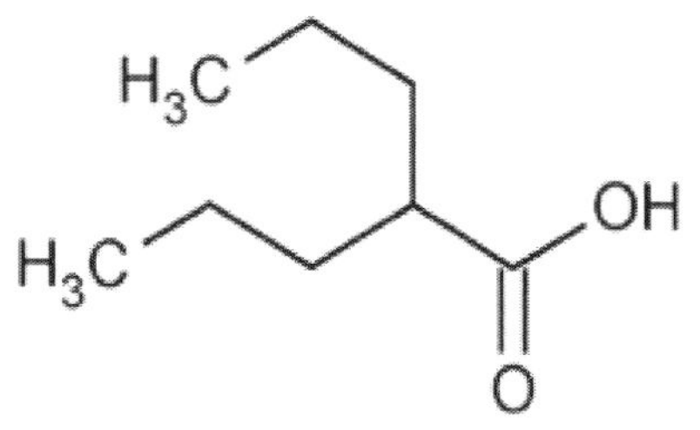

This is the only structure with the correct molecular formula, $C_8H_{16}O_2$, and a carboxylic acid functional group (hence the name 'acid').

Structures 3 and 4 have incorrect molecular formulas, and structures 2 and 5 lack a carboxylic acid functional group and would not be weakly acidic.

6.

(a), x = 5

The mass of hydrated copper sulfate heated is (28.00 - 19.02) = 8.98 g.

The mass of anhydrous copper sulfate obtained is (24.76-19.02) = 5.74 g.

Anhydrous copper sulfate has a molar mass of 159.61 g/mol

$$5.74 \text{ g}/159.61 \text{ g/mol} = 0.0359 \text{ mol } CuSO_4$$

The amount of water lost by heating is (8.98 - 5.74) = 3.24 g

The number of moles of water lost is

$$3.24 \text{ g} / 18.02 \text{ g/mol} = 0.180 \text{ mol}$$

The ratio of the number of moles of water to the number of moles of copper sulfate is:

$$0.180 / 0.0359 = 5.01, \text{ or 5 moles water per mole copper sulfate.}$$

So x = 5

(b) The weight after the first heating is not constant, i.e. after further heating the weight is reduced significantly. This is because the reaction is not complete - not all the water has been removed by heating. If this weight were used in the calculations above, the mass of water lost would appear to be reduced and the mass of 'anhydrous' copper sulfate left would be increased. This would result in the calculated x being lower than the correct value.

(c) The hydration reaction is exothermic, because heat is evolved. The reverse reaction must therefore be endothermic, hence the need to heat the hydrated copper sulfate to drive the water off.

7.

(a) - the balanced redox equation is:

$$MnO_4^- + 8H^+ + 5Fe^{2+} \rightarrow Mn^{2+} + 5Fe^{3+} + 4H_2O$$

(b) - First, calculate amount of permanganate used:

0.01208 L x 0.200 mol/L = 2.42 x 10^{-3} moles MnO_4^-

Next, calculate amount of iron present. According to the equation, the ratio of MnO_4^- : Fe^{2+} is 1:5, so:

2.42 x 10^{-3} moles x 5/1 = 1.21 x 10^{-2} moles Fe^{2+}

The aliquot of iron solution was 10.0 mL, from a total volume of 100.0 mL. So the total number of moles of iron in the nail is:

1.21 x 10^{-2} moles x 100.0 mL/10.0 mL = 1.21 x 10^{-1} moles , or 0.121 moles Fe

Mass of iron in initial sample:

0.121 moles x 55.85 g/mol = 0.675 g

(c) - The mass of iron in the sample is 0.675 g. The total mass is 0.750 g. The purity is:

0.675 g/0.75 g = 90.0 %

(d) - An impurity that reacted with permanganate would increase the volume of permanganate solution required to oxidize the iron. This would overestimate the amount of iron present, which would result in an overestimate of the purity of the iron.

You won't be able to use a calculator on the multiple choice questions in this exam – just pencil and paper (you can use a calculator on the Free Response questions, though.) Also, you won't find detailed explanations in the Answer Key – that's because the principles are covered in detail in the previous two. It's time you started learning to synthesize all this information; good luck!

Multiple Choice Questions

1. **A hot air balloon has an approximate volume of 50,000 cubic meters at sea-level, where the pressure is 1 atmosphere. If the balloon rises to 10,000 feet, where the pressure is approximately 0.6 atmospheres, what will the new volume of the balloon?**
    a. 65,000 cubic meters
    b. 80,000 cubic meters
    c. 83,333 cubic meters
    d. 91,666 cubic meters

Questions 2 through 3 are based on the following reaction system.

$$NiO_2 + 2\ H_2O + Fe \longrightarrow Ni(OH)_2 + Fe(OH)_2 \text{ in acidic solution}$$

2. **What is the balanced half-reaction for nickel in this reaction system, and what is the net change in oxidation state of nickel?**
    a. $NiO_2 + 2H_2O \rightarrow Ni(OH)_2 + O_2$, +2 oxidation state
    b. $NiO_2 + 2H_2O + 2e\text{-} \rightarrow Ni(OH)_2 + O_2 + H_2$, -2 oxidation state
    c. $NiO_2 + 2e\text{-} + 2H+ \rightarrow Ni(OH)_2$, -2 oxidation state
    d. $NiO_2 + H_2O + 2e\text{-} \rightarrow Ni(OH)_2$, -4 oxidation state

3. **If 0.25 mols of nickel oxide is consumed in the reaction, how many grams of nickel hydroxide will be produced?**
    a. 23.2 grams
    b. 24.5 grams
    c. 17.8 grams
    d. 29.5 grams

4. Given the two molecules seen below, which of the following statements is true?

A   B

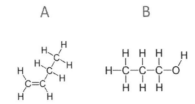

   a. Molecule A has a lower boiling point than molecule B because it is a more polar molecule.
   b. Molecule A has a higher boiling point than molecule B because it is more sterically hindered.
   c. Molecule B has a higher boiling point than molecule A because it is a more polar molecule.
   d. Molecule B has a lower boiling point than molecule A because it has fewer carbons and a lower molecular weight.

5. The Haber-Bosch process uses the chemical reaction seen below to create ammonia out of nitrogen and hydrogen gas. At 500 °C, the reaction only goes to 82% completion. Which of the following could *not* be used to drive the reaction equilibrium further to the right?

$$N_2 + 3\,H_2 \rightarrow 2\,NH_3$$

   a. Increasing the temperature
   b. Increasing the pressure
   c. Adding a catalyst
   d. Increasing the concentrations of nitrogen and hydrogen gas

6. Which of the following molecules does not have an ionic bond?
   a. $FeCl_2$
   b. H_3PO_4
   c. KOH
   d. C_2H_6

7. In the phase diagram below, which point represents the transition from solid to liquid?

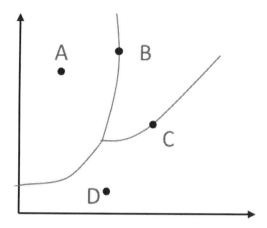

   a. A
   b. B
   c. C
   d. D

8. A student wishes to conduct an experiment to determine the heat of reaction for a particular reaction. Which of the following equipment would they need?
   a. A bomb calorimeter
   b. A burette
   c. A galvanic cell
   d. A gravimetric analyzer

9. Citric acid has a pKa of 3.14 for its first proton and a pKa of 4.71 for its second proton at room temperature. Which of the following is true if a scientist wishes to use citric acid to make a buffer?
   a. A citric acid buffer is effective from pH 3 to pH 9.
   b. A citric acid buffer is effective from pH 3 to pH 5.
   c. A citric acid buffer should be mixed with another strong acid in order to form the buffer solution.
   d. A citric acid buffer should be mixed with an equal molar portion of a strong base in order to form the buffer solution.

10. Which of the following reaction energy diagrams shows a reaction with the highest activation energy?

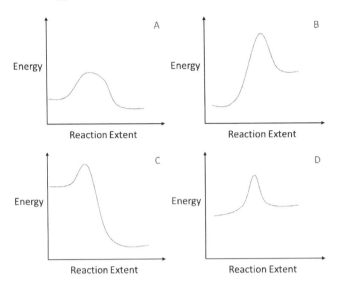

a. A
b. B
c. C
d. D

11. A scientist analyzed a molecule of ethane (C_2H_6) and discovered that the carbon-carbon bond in the molecule has a bond dissociation energy of 350 kJ/mol, and a length of 1.55 angstroms. He then examines a molecule of ethene (C_2H_4). Which of the following should be true about his findings?

a. He will find that the ethene C-C bond strength is less than the ethane molecule.
b. He will find that the ethene C-C bond length is greater than the ethane molecule.
c. He will find that the ethene C-C bond strength is greater than the ethane molecule.
d. He will find that the ethene C-C bond strength is greater, and the bond length shorter, than the ethane molecule.

12. What is the reaction quotient for the reaction below?

$$NO + O_3 \leftrightarrow NO_2 + O_2$$

There are currently 0.25 mols NO, 0.15 mols O_3, 1.5 mols NO_2, and 1.2 mols of O_2.

    a. 12
    b. 24
    c. 48
    d. 64

13. A catalyst is a substance that can be used to reduce the amount of energy needed to start a reaction, or the activation energy. Which of the following lines on the reaction energy diagram below represents a reaction which has a catalyst present, assuming the red line is the original reaction?

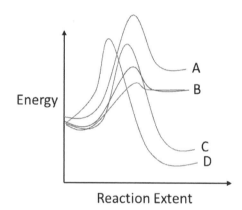

    a. A
    b. B
    c. C
    d. D

Questions 14 to 16 are based on the following information.

The solubility of a compound is determined by many factors, including the presence of a similar ion in solution, the temperature, and in some cases, the partial pressure of the gas above the solution. Calcium hydroxide is a compound that dissolves relatively easily into water, and its solubility can be represented by:

$$S = 1/2[OH-]_{ethanol}$$

Thus, by measuring the content of OH- ions in solution through titration, we can determine the overall solubility of calcium hydroxide in that solvent.

However, calcium hydroxide's solubility can be influenced by the presence of a similar ion. Its solubility will thus decrease accordingly. Its new solubility is represented by:

$$S = \frac{1}{2}\{[OH]_{total} - [OH]_{solvent}\}$$

14. A student performs a titration on a 1 liter solution of ethanol containing 0.5 mols of calcium hydroxide. He calculates that 0.46 mols of a strong acid, HCl, are required to neutralize the solution. The solubility of calcium hydroxide in ethanol in this experiment is:
    a. 0.23 mols/liter
    b. 0.31 mols/liter
    c. 0.46 mols/liter
    d. 0.50 mols/liter

15. Which of the following methods could be used to increase the solubility of Ca(OH)$_2$ in ethanol?
    a. Adding OH- ions to the solution
    b. Removing OH- ions from the solution
    c. Adding more water to the solution
    d. Stirring the solution vigorously

16. A student wishes to measure the solubility of the compound Copper (III) hydroxide in water. The solubility equation for this compound might look like:
    a. $S = [OH-]$
    b. $S = 2 [OH-]$
    c. $S = 1/3 [OH-]$
    d. $S = ¼ [OH-]$

17. The latent heat of vaporization of ammonia is about $1/20^{th}$ that of water. This means that if water and ammonia are both at their boiling points, which of the following statements is true?
    a. Ammonia will require 20 times more energy to turn into vapor compared to water.
    b. Ammonia will require 20 times more energy to see an increase of 1 degree in temperature compared to water.
    c. Water will require 20 times more energy to turn into vapor compared to ammonia.
    d. Water will require 20 times more energy to see an increase of 1 degree in temperature compared to ammonia.

18. A student has determined that a reaction has run to equilibrium. If this is true, then:
    a. $K = Q$
    b. $K < Q$
    c. $K > Q$
    d. $K + Q = 1$

Questions 19 to 20 refer to the following information.

The reaction of silver nitration with a basic molecule results in the formation of a dark silver oxide compound. The reaction is given below.

$$AgNO_3 + NaOH \rightarrow Ag_2O + NaNO_3 + H_2O \quad \Delta H = -34.5 \text{ kJ/mol}$$

19. Which of the following is the correct balanced reaction equation?
    a. $2 AgNO_3 + 2 NaOH \rightarrow Ag_2O + 2 NaNO_3 + H_2O$
    b. $4 AgNO_3 + 3 NaOH \rightarrow Ag_2O + 2 NaNO_3 + H_2O$
    c. $AgNO_3 + 2 NaOH \rightarrow Ag_2O + 2 NaNO_3 + H_2O$
    d. $2 AgNO_3 + 2 NaOH \rightarrow 2 Ag_2O + 2 NaNO_3 + H_2O$

255

20. In the balanced reaction, if 0.5 mols of silver nitrate are consumed in the reaction, how much heat is produced or consumed?
    a. 17.25 kJ consumed
    b. 34.5 kJ consumed
    c. 17.25 kJ produced
    d. 17.25 kJ produced

21. What is the correct name for Na_2SO_4?
    a. Disodium sulfite
    b. Disodium sulfur oxide
    c. Sodium sulfate
    d. Sodium (II) sulfate

22. Lithium is an unstable element in its pure form. If left by itself in air, it will eventually spontaneously combust and form lithium oxide. Which of the following is true regarding this reaction?
    a. The reaction is very favorable and driven by a change from low entropy to high entropy
    b. The reaction is moderately favorable and driven by an enthalpy change
    c. The reaction is not very favorable and requires both a high input of heat and change in entropy
    d. The reaction is not favorable and requires a change in enthalpy, in addition to the presence of oxygen as a catalyst.

23. A student burns 5 grams of an unknown sample of hydrocarbon, C_xH_y. She produces 11 grams of carbon dioxide. Assuming the reaction went to completion (all the hydrocarbon was combusted), what was the mass of carbon in the original sample?
    a. 0.25 grams
    b. 2.50 grams
    c. 3.00 grams
    d. 3.15 grams

24. In the following reaction, which species is being reduced?

$$2\ MnO_4- + 5\ SO_3^{2-} + 6\ H^+ \rightarrow 2\ Mn^{2+} + 5\ SO_4^{2-} + 3\ H_2O$$

 a. Manganese
 b. Sulfur
 c. Oxygen
 d. Hydrogen

25. Which of the following molecules can act as both an acid and a base?
 a. HCl
 b. HSO_3^-
 c. NH_4
 d. NO_3^-

Questions 26 to 28 refer to the following information.

A weak acid is being titrated with a strong base, NaOH at 0.100 molarity. The titration chart below shows the information gathered.

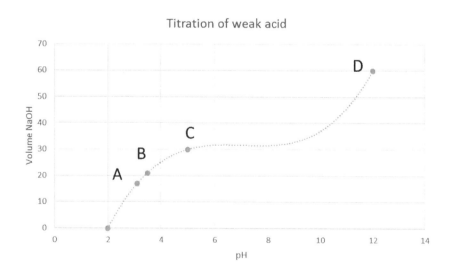

26. What is the approximate pH of the half-equivalence point of this acid?
 a. 5.5
 b. 7
 c. 8.5
 d. 10

27. At point A on the titration curve, which species should have the highest concentration in solution?
    a. H+
    b. OH-
    c. Na+
    d. NO_3-

28. Approximately how much more base would need to be added before the equivalence point is reached?
    a. 20 mL
    b. 40 mL
    c. 60 mL
    d. 80 mL

29. Uranium 233 has a half-life of about 70 years. If an area is contaminated with this compound, how long will it take to reach less than 5% of its original concentration? Round to the nearest number.
    a. 3 half lives
    b. 4 half lives
    c. 5 half lives
    d. 6 half lives

30. In the nuclear reaction shown below, what is the missing product?

$$^{11}_{5}B \rightarrow product + {}^{4}_{2}He$$

    a. $^{9}_{5}B$
    b. $^{7}_{5}Li$
    c. $^{7}_{3}Li$
    d. $^{9}_{3}B$

31. A student conducts an experiment to determine the oxidation state of a sample of aluminum that she has found. She succeeds in dissolving a small amount of the ionic compound into aqueous solution, and finds that there is a 3:2 ratio of oxygen to aluminum in the sample. The oxidation state of aluminum is:
    a. -2
    b. -3
    c. +2
    d. +3

32. Which of the following compounds is the least soluble in water?
    a. Na_2SO_4
    b. $Ca(OH)_2$
    c. MnS
    d. NH_4OH

33. Which of the following statements is not true regarding the halogens in the periodic table?
    a. All of the halogens are extremely reactive.
    b. The halogen elements require 1 more electron to fill their valence shell.
    c. Halogen elements usually form ionic bonds with other elements.
    d. All of the halogens are very electronegative, except for Astatine and Iodine.

34. A student mixes 400 mL of a 0.50 molar $Pb(NO_3)_2$ solution with 200 mL of a 0.8 molar $MgCl_2$ solution. What will be the final amount of lead ions present in the solution?
    a. 0.04 mols
    b. 0.16 mols
    c. 0.20 mols
    d. 0.28 mols

Questions 35 to 36 are based on the following information.

The reaction below has an equilibrium constant of Kc = 0.15

$$Cu + 2AgNO_3 \rightarrow 2Ag + Cu(NO_3)_2$$

35. If 1 mol of copper and 1 mol of silver nitrate are present initially, what is the approximate amount of silver formed?
    a. 0.42 mols
    b. 0.84 mols
    c. 1 mol
    d. 1.15 mols

36. Separately, if 1 mol of copper and 1 mol of silver nitrate are present initially, what is the limiting reagent and how much of the excess reagent will be remaining, assuming the reaction goes to completion?
    a. Copper, 0.5 mols
    b. Copper, 1 mol
    c. Silver nitrate, 0.5 mols
    d. Silver nitrate, 1 mol

37. Which of the following elements has the highest first ionization energy?
    a. Sodium
    b. Sulfur
    c. Carbon
    d. Argon

38. A scientist has a 0.50 liter solution of 0.5 molar potassium chloride (KCl). He wishes to make a 1 liter solution that has a 1 molarity concentration of chlorine ions. Which of the following should he add?
    a. 0.5 liters of a 0.5 molar NaCl solution.
    b. 0.5 liters of a 1 molar NaCl solution.
    c. 0.5 liters of a 1 molar KCl solution.
    d. 0.5 liters of a 1.5 molar KCl solution.

39. The electron configuration for Phosphorus is:
    a. $1s^2 2s^2 2p^6 3s^2 3p^3$
    b. $1s^2 2s^2 2p^6 3s^2 3p^6$
    c. $1s^2 2p^6 3s^2 3p^3$
    d. $1s^2 2s^2 2p^2 3s^2 3p^3 4s^2 4p^3$

Questions 40 to 42 are based on the information below.

The four molecules below all have similar molecular weights, but possess different functional groups and properties.

A

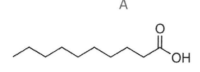

B

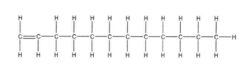

C

D

40. Which of these molecules are acidic?
    a. A only
    b. A and B
    c. B and D
    d. A, B, and C

41. Based on their structures, which molecule should have the highest boiling point?
    a. A
    b. B
    c. C
    d. D

42. Which of these molecules will have the strongest intermolecular bonding interactions?
    a. A
    b. B
    c. C
    d. A and B will have equal strength bonding interactions.

43. In a kinetics experiment for a simple reaction A + B → C + D, which of the following would indicate that the reaction is of second order?
   a. An increase in the concentration of reactants leads to a doubling of the formation of product.
   b. The rate law has a constant equal to 2.
   c. The rate law exponents add up to 2.
   d. An increase in the concentration of reactants results in a linear increase in the formation of products.

44. At room temperature, the reaction below is not spontaneous, and occurs at a very slow rate. However, as the temperature decreases toward 0 Kelvin, the reaction rate increases, eventually becoming spontaneous around 40 K. This indicates that the reaction is:

$$2 \ Al(s) + 3 \ Cl_2(g) \rightarrow 2 \ AlCl_3(s)$$

   a. Has a positive ΔH value
   b. Has a negative ΔH value
   c. Has a negative S value and a positive ΔH value
   d. None of the above

45. A catalyst is designed to:
   a. Increase the amount of energy released during the course of a reaction
   b. Increase the amount of energy consumed during the course of a reaction
   c. Reduce the activation energy required for a reaction
   d. Lower the entropy change that occurs during a reaction

46. In the diagram below, which depicts the titration of a weak diprotic acid with a strong base, what does the indicated point show?

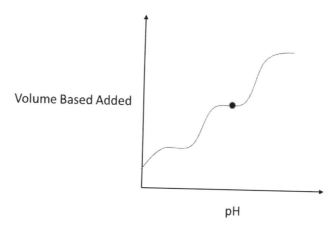

a. The basic equivalence point of the first proton
b. The equivalence point of the second proton
c. The point at which HA = A- for the first proton
d. The half equivalence point of the second proton

47. A student has accidentally spilled 2 liters of a 0.5 molar solution of a weak acid. How much NaOH is needed to neutralize this spill?
a. 0.5 mols
b. 1 mol
c. 1.5 mols
d. There is not enough information given to answer this question

Questions 48 to 50 are based on the following information.

A student is performing an experiment in which she wants to measure the kinetic rate of the reaction shown below:

$$CH_3COOH \text{ (aq)} + NaHCO_3 \text{ (s)} \rightarrow CH_3COONa \text{ (aq)} + CO_2 \text{ (g)} + H_2O \text{ (l)}$$

In order to perform this experiment, she first mixes 200 mL of a 0.5 molar solution of CH_3COOH. She then places 21 grams of sodium bicarbonate into the solution to start the reaction.

48. Which of the following laboratory glassware would be the most appropriate for use in making the CH_3COOH solution?

    a. A 500 mL Erlenmeyer flask with 20 mL graduations

    b. A 500 mL beaker with 20 mL graduations

    c. A 200 mL volumetric flask

    d. A 100 mL graduated cylinder with 5 mL graduations

49. What is the limiting reagent in this reaction?

    a. CH_3COOH

    b. $NaHCO_3$

    c. The two reagents are present in equal molar amounts

    d. H_2O

50. Which of the following techniques could she *not* use to measure the extent of the reaction?

    a. Collection of CO2 gas to discover the mass of CO2 produced.

    b. Analysis of the product solution with UV spectra to determine the concentration of CH_3COONa

    c. Using titration to find the concentration of OH- ions produced.

    d. Removing the residual solid $NaHCO_3$ and finding its mass.

51. In the reaction given below, which of the following statements is true?

$$CO_3{}^{2-} + 2H^+ \rightarrow CO_2 + H_2O$$

    a. Carbon is being oxidized

    b. Oxygen is being reduced

    c. Hydrogen and oxygen are being reduced

    d. Neither carbon nor oxygen have a change in oxidation state

52. Alyssa digs up a lump of iron (II) oxide, and finds that its mass is 162 grams. How many mols of iron are in this lump?

    a. 1 mol

    b. 1.5 mols

    c. 2 mols

    d. 3 mols

53. Metals are conductive materials that are able to transfer electrons through the atoms in the compound. Which of these elements is the most conductive?
   a. Scandium
   b. Manganese
   c. Boron
   d. Calcium

54. Alex finds a compound that is determined to be 50.1% copper, 16.3% phosphorus, and 33.6% oxygen. What could a possible molecular formula for this compound be?
   a. Cu_2PO_3
   b. $CuPO$
   c. $Cu_3(PO_4)_2$
   d. $CuPO_4$

55. A scientist wishes to add a halogen to an octane molecule, seen below, to form 1-X-octane. He wants the reaction rate to be as fast as possible. Which halogen should he use?

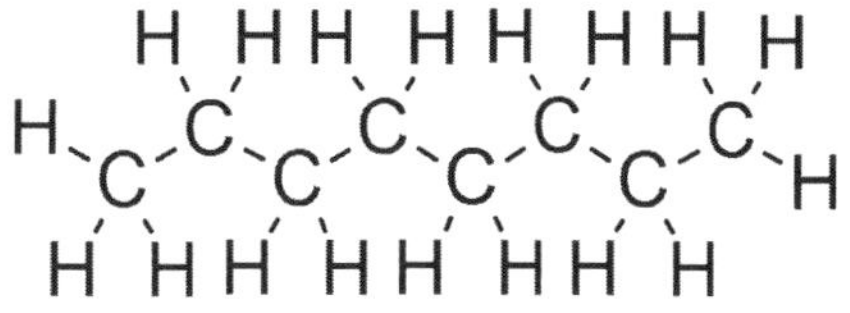

   a. Fluorine
   b. Bromine
   c. Chlorine
   d. Astatine

56. The elements in the 18th group of the periodic table are not very reactive. This can be explained by the fact that they:
   a. All have high atomic masses
   b. All have average electronegativity values
   c. Are all present in diatomic form naturally, preventing easy access for reaction.
   d. Do not have any unpaired electrons

57. Jet fuel used in planes is typically a 15 carbon hydrocarbon, in the form of $C_{15}H_{32}$. If a plane burns 200 mols of this fuel, approximately how much water is produced?
   a. 20 kilograms
   b. 40 kilograms
   c. 60 kilograms
   d. 85 kilograms

58. Which of the statements below correctly distinguish between a homogenous reaction and a heterogeneous reaction?
   a. A homogenous reaction has the same number of products as reactants whereas a heterogeneous reaction does not.
   b. A homogenous reaction does not require heat whereas a heterogeneous reaction does.
   c. A homogenous reaction has all reactants in the same phase, whereas a heterogeneous reaction does not.
   d. All of the above are true.

59. In order to assess an experiment that can measure the reaction rate, K, of a reaction, which reaction equation is necessary?
   a. Van Der Waal's extent equation
   b. Arrhenius' equation
   c. Charles' Law
   d. Le Chatelier's equation

60. Pure sodium reacts with water according to the following equation. If 2 grams of sodium are placed in 100 mL of water, and after 5 seconds 0.4 grams of sodium remain, what was the average rate of reaction?

$$2\ Na + 2\ H_2O \rightarrow 2\ NaOH + H_2$$

   a. 0.16 g/sec
   b. 0.32 g/sec
   c. 0.39 g/sec
   d. 0.41 g/sec

Free Response Questions

There are four short response questions and three long response questions. The use of a calculator is permitted.

1. A student is performing an experiment to determine the energy contained in gasoline, which is 90% octane and 10% hexane, by mol ratio.

    a. Write the complete balanced reaction equations for the combustion of octane and hexane individually.

    b. Calculate the volume of air at STP required to completely combust 100 mol of gasoline. Assume that air is 21% by mol oxygen.

    c. Describe and draw an experiment that could be used to determine the heat of reaction for this combustion reaction.

2. For each of the following three reactions, write the complete balanced reaction, including phase, and answer the question associated.
    a. A solution of cadmium sulfate is mixed with a solution of potassium sulfide.
        i. If 1 mol of each reactant was used, what is the limiting reagent?

    b. A student titrates a solution of potassium hydroxide of an unknown concentration with a 0.1M nitric acid solution.
        i. The student uses bromomethyl blue as an indicator, which is yellow at low pH and blue at high pH. What is the color of the solution at the half-equivalence point?

    c. Elemental iron is left out in the air for several days, and forms a coat of rust.
        i. What are the possible oxidation states of oxygen in this reaction?

3. **Based on the depiction of the galvanic cell below, answer the following questions.**

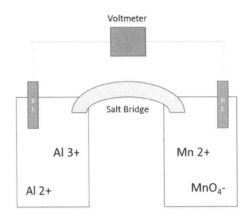

Half reaction	e(V)
Al 3+ + e- → Al 2+	-0.062
MnO_4- + 8 H+ + 5 e- → Mn2+ + 4 H2O(l)	+1.490

a. Write the complete balanced equation for this redox reaction, and calculate the standard potential.

b. On the diagram, label the anode and the cathode.

c. What is the number of mols of electrons that are produced or consumed if 2 mols of MnO_4 are used in the reaction?

4. Based on the structures of the three acids seen below, answer the following questions.

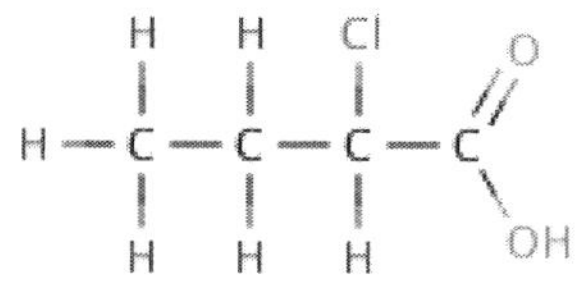

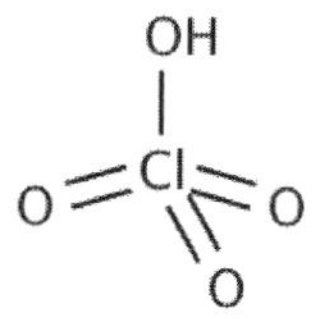

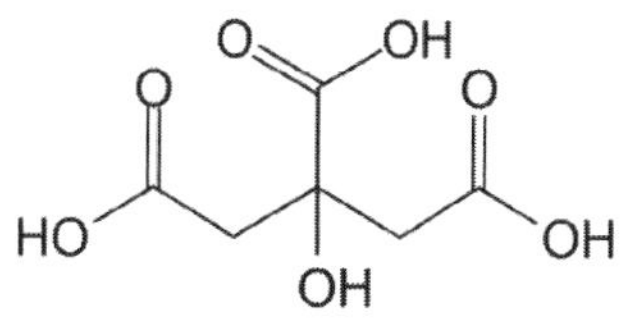

a. Which of the acids is the strongest and why?

b. Are any of these acids amphoteric, and if so, under what conditions might they be amphoteric?

5. In the reaction below, an acid is combining with an alcohol molecule to form an ester.

$$CH_3CH_2COOH + CH_3CH_2OH \rightarrow CH_3CH_2COOCH_2CH_3 + H_2O$$

a. What are the IUPAC names for the reactants and the products?

b. Draw the structure of the acid reactant. Also, state the hybridization/VSEPR structure of the acidic carbon and the number of pi bonds that it possesses.

c. The acid reagent is soluble in water, and the entire reaction takes place in the aqueous state. However, a molecule that is very similar in structure, $CH_3CH_2CH_3$, is not soluble. Explain the difference in solubility.

6. The following subset of questions can be answered by referring to the periodic table.

    a. Based on the known atomic radius of Selenium of 1.15 angstroms, what would a predicted atomic radius for Germanium be, and why?

    b. Br_2 is a compound that has purely covalent bond with a bond dissociation energy of 193 kJ/mol. Predict three other binary compounds consisting of 2 elements each that should have a higher bond dissociation energy than Br_2, and explain why.

    c. Platinum is a metal that is used for catalysis. However, platinum is extremely expensive. What might be a good substitute for platinum as a catalyst and why?

7. A student is working on an experiment to determine the rate constant of the reaction seen below:

$$N_2H_4(l) + O_2(g) \rightarrow N_2(g) + 2\ H_2O(g)$$

    a. Describe this experiment and what equipment would be needed.

    b. According to the Arrhenius Equation, seen below, what would happen to the reaction if the temperature was increased by a factor of 4? Explain your reasoning as well.

$$k = Ae^{\frac{-Ea}{RT}}$$

1.	C	31.	D
2.	C	32.	C
3.	A	33.	D
4.	C	34.	A
5.	D	35.	B
6.	D	36.	C
7.	B	37.	D
8.	A	38.	D
9.	B	39.	A
10.	C	40.	D
11.	D	41.	B
12.	C	42.	B
13.	B	43.	C
14.	A	44.	B
15.	B	45.	C
16.	C	46.	D
17.	C	47.	D
18.	A	48.	C
19.	A	49.	A
20.	C	50.	C
21.	C	51.	D
22.	B	52.	C
23.	C	53.	B
24.	A	54.	C
25.	B	55.	A
26.	B	56.	D
27.	A	57.	C
28.	A	58.	C
29.	C	59.	B
30.	C	60.	B

Answer Key: Free Response

Free Response Questions

1. This problem tests the student's ability to write balanced equations and to use the ideal gas law.

    a. In part A, the balanced reactions of hexane and octane need to be written to show the formation of CO_2 and water as a byproduct. They should look like:

        $C_6H_{14} + 13\ O_2 \rightarrow 6\ CO_2 + 7\ H_2O$

        $C_8H_{18} + 17\ O_2 \rightarrow 8\ CO_2 + 9\ H_2O$

        The student needs to correctly balance the addition of oxygen into the reaction.

    b. This one is a bit tricky. First of all, the student needs calculate the number of mols of each fuel. There is 90 mols of octane and 10 mols of hexane.

        According to the stoichiometry solved in part A, 1 mol of hexane requires 13 mols of oxygen, and one mol of hexane requires 17 mols of oxygen.

        Thus, 13x10 + 17*90 = 1660 mols of oxygen required.

        Air is 21% by mol oxygen, and thus, about 7900 mols of air is required. The volume of air at STP is 22.4 liters per mol. If the student does not know this as fact, it can be shown through the ideal gas law.

    c. This results in 176,960 liters of air needed. Rounded answers can be accepted, as long as work is shown.

    d. In part C, it is expected that the student is able to write at least one paragraph explaining the use of a bomb calorimeter.

2. This question tests the students' knowledge of chemical names and writing reaction equations based on the names.

   a. Cadmium sulfate is $CdSO_4$ and Potassium sulfide is K_2S. The reaction is:

      i. $CdSO_4 + K_2S \rightarrow CdS + K_2SO_4$. There is no limiting reagent if 1 mol of each compound is used, because the stoichiometric ratio of reagents is 1:1.

   b. Potassium hydroxide is KOH and nitric acid is HNO_3. The reaction is:

      i. $KOH + HNO_3 \rightarrow KNO_3 + H_2O$. Because KOH is a strong base and nitric acid is only a moderately strong acid, at the half equivalence point the pH should still be basic. This means that the indicator should still be blue.

   c. Fe is iron and oxygen is O_2. There are two possible reactions. The student needs to write just one down.

      i. $4\,Fe + 3O_2 \rightarrow Fe_2O_3$
      ii. $Fe + O \rightarrow FeO$
      iii. The possible oxidation states of iron are +2 and +3 in these reactions.

3. The student needs to show the process of constructing the complete half reaction by first combining the two half reactions, and then showing the steps of balancing the reaction.

   In the complete reaction, there **should not** be any electron species present if the reaction is properly balanced. The electron species are only shown in the half reactions.

   On the diagram, we note that manganese is being reduced. The site of reduction in a galvanic cell, or where the electrons are going, is the cathode. The site of oxidation, in this case, the aluminum, is the anode.

   Finally, if 2 mols of MnO4 are consumed from the reaction, we can see that one mol of MnO4 results in the transfer of 5 electrons. Thus 2 mols will result in the transfer of 10 mols of electrons.

4. This question tests the student's ability to correlate structural differences in molecules into chemical properties.

   a. The strongest acid is the one in which a negative charge can be best stabilized by its conjugate base. The double bonds in the perchloric acid molecule (the middle one) allow for the best resonance stabilization of a negative charge. As a result, that is the strongest acid.

   b. The acid on the far right is amphoteric. An amphoteric molecule is able to act as an acid or a base. Because this acid (citric acid) has 3 protons that it can donate, it has a possibility of acting as an amphoteric compound. However, it can only be amphoteric once it has lost at least one proton. If all protons are present, then the molecule is acidic only.

5. This question tests the student's knowledge of VSEPR structure and electron bonding.

   a. The name of the acid is ethanoic acid. Acetic acid, the common name, is not accepted. The name of the alcohol is ethanol. The common name, ethyl alcohol, is not accepted.

   b. The structure of the acid is seen below:

   There is just one pi bond in this structure, due to there being just a single double pond. Bonus points if the student also mentions that there are 3 sigma bonds and differentiates between a sigma bond and a pi bond.

   The acidic carbon has no free electrons and has a steric number of 3. The double bond with oxygen has higher electron density, so this is not a trigonal planar molecule. It is best described as a bent configuration.

6. This tests the student's knowledge of chemical properties based on the periodic table.

    a. Selenium is element 34, and germanium is 32. The student should mention that atomic radius is directly proportional to electron shells in an element. Germanium has 2 less electrons than selenium, but the same number of electron shells. As such, the atomic radius of germanium should be only a little smaller than selenium. We can predict a radius of 1.12 or 1.10 angstroms.

    b. The student can pick any three highly ionic bonds. Ionic bonds between elements with high electronegativity value differences always have a stronger bond strength than single covalent bonds. Examples could be KCl, $MgBr_2$, or FeO.

    c. The function of a catalyst depends on its electron structure. The student can pick any metal that is adjacent to platinum on the periodic table. This includes gold, palladium, iridium, or rhodium.

7. For the first part, the student needs to describe an experiment in which at least 3 trials are run. Each trial should have a varying concentration of the different reagents.

For the second part, the student should explain that because the temperature is an inverse correlation (1/T) and in the exponent of the equation, increasing the temperature by a factor of 4 would still increase the reaction rate, but probably only by 30 or 40%. Using a calculator they can demonstrate this by choosing arbitrary values of Ea, activation energy.

Practice Examination 4

On this one, like on exam 3, don't use a calculator for the multiple-choice questions. If you cheat and use one now, you won't have the ability to do these problems on the actual examination, so the only person you're hurting is yourself.

Multiple Choice Questions

1. **Shari is working in lab on a reaction that involves two reagents. She finds that if she adds more of reagent A, there is no increase in the rate of reaction. If she adds more of reagent B, there is an exponential increase in the rate of reaction. Accordingly, she can conclude that:**
   a. Reagent A has a rate law of zero, and reagent B has a rate law of 1.
   b. Reagent A has a rate law of 1, and reagent B has a rate law of 2.
   c. Reagent A has a rate law of 0, and reagent B has a rate law of 2.
   d. Both reagent A and reagent B have rate laws of 1.

2. **In a given reaction, the reaction quotient was found to be 200% of the equilibrium constant. this means that:**
   a. The reaction will proceed to the right
   b. The reaction is at equilibrium
   c. The reaction is at completion
   d. The reaction will proceed to the left

Questions 3 and 4 refer to the following substances listed below.

H_2O $C_6H_{12}O_6$ HF CH_3CH_2OH C_2H_6

3. **Which of these substances is the only non-polar compound?**
   a. $C_6H_{12}O_6$
   b. HF
   c. C_2H_6
   d. H_2O

4. Which of these substances is the most acidic?
    a. HF
    b. CH_3CH_2OH
    c. H_2O
    d. $C_6H_{12}O_6$

5. In a 0.5 liter solution of 0.2M $NaNO_3$ and 1M NaCl, what is the mass of sodium ions?
    a. 11 grams
    b. 14 grams
    c. 18 grams
    d. 21 grams

6. For the reaction given below, what is the correct rate law equation?

$$2\ NO + Br_2 \rightarrow 2NOBr$$

    a. Rate = k[NO][Br]
    b. Rate = k[NOBr]
    c. Rate = $k[NO]^2[Br][NOBr]^2$
    d. Rate = $k[NO]^2[Br]$

7. The electron configuration of bromine in its ionized state is most nearly:
    a. [Ar] $4s^2\ 3d^{10}\ 4p^5$
    b. [Ne] $4s^2\ 3d^{10}\ 4p^6$
    c. [Ar] $4s^2\ 4p^5$
    d. [Kr]

8. What is the correct name for the compound HCN?
    a. Hydrocarbonitride
    b. Hydrogen cyanide
    c. Hydrogen cyanonitride
    d. Cyanonitrile hydride

9. A molecule has the formula XY_2, and two pairs of non-bonding electrons. Its hybridization and shape should be classified as:
   a. sp^2, linear
   b. sp^3, trigonal planar
   c. dsp^2, seesaw
   d. sp^3, bent

10. At room temperature and pressure, the volume of a gas sample is 20 liters. If the temperature is doubled, what is the new volume, assuming pressure remains constant?
    a. 30 liters
    b. 40 liters
    c. 60 liters
    d. 80 liters

11. Hexane (C_6H_{14}) is significantly more soluble in carbon tetrachloride than it is in water. What is the explanation for this difference?
    a. Hexane and carbon tetrachloride have more similar molecular masses.
    b. Hexane and carbon tetrachloride are both non-polar molecules.
    c. Hexane and water have boiling points that are too different.
    d. Water does not have any carbon atoms, but hexane does.

12. In a gas synthesis reaction, seen below, 29.5 liters of product gas were produced at STP. What is the mass of product produced?

$$2\ CO(g) + O_2(g) \rightarrow 2CO_2(g)$$

    a. 31 grams
    b. 44 grams
    c. 58 grams
    d. 64 grams

13. A scientist has created a buffer solution out of acetic acid and sodium acetate. The pH of the buffer solution is 4.5 and the molarity is 1. If 200 mL of 0.5 molar NaOH is added to a 1 liter solution of the buffer, what will happen to the pH?
    a. It will increase to 5.0.
    b. It will decrease to around 3.9.
    c. It will increase to the pH of sodium hydroxide, which is 12.
    d. It will remain the same.

14. Anne wishes to calculate the number of mols of gas that are present in her bedroom. She knows that the temperature of her bedroom is 26°C and the volume is approximately 30 cubic meters. Which of the following pieces of information could she use to solve this problem?
    a. The type of molecules present in the air in her room.
    b. The percentage of oxygen in the air.
    c. The height of her room above sea level and the corresponding pressure.
    d. All of the above are necessary to solve this problem.

15. Prior to beginning a titration of a weak acid with a strong base, the buret needs to be cleaned and rinsed with:
    a. Distilled water
    b. Ethanol
    c. A sample of the strong base
    d. A sample of the weak acid

16. In the following oxidation reduction reaction, what is the net change in oxidation state of chromium?

$$Cr_2O_7{}^{2-}(aq) + HNO_2(aq) \rightarrow Cr^{3+}(aq) + NO_3{}^-(aq)$$

    a. +3
    b. -3
    c. +4
    d. -4

Questions 17 to 19 refer to the following information.

The reaction of magnesium chloride and sodium sulfate follows the reaction below:

$$MgCl_2 + Na_2SO_4 \rightarrow MgSO_4 + 2NaCl \quad \Delta H = -17.2 \text{ kJ/mol}$$

At the start of the reaction, there is 1 mol of magnesium chloride and 1 mol of sodium sulfate. There are 0 mols of product.

17. What is the equilibrium constant equation for this reaction?

a. $k = \dfrac{[MgSO4][NaCl]^2}{[MgCl2][Na2SO4]}$

b. $k = [MgSO4][NaCl]$

c. $k = \dfrac{2[MgSO4][NaCl]}{[MgCl2][Na2SO4]}$

d. $k = \dfrac{[MgSO4]^2[NaCl]}{[MgCl2][Na2SO4]}$

18. Given the fact that the equilibrium constant for this reaction is 0.17, what is the correct equation that we should solve in order to obtain the final concentrations of product?

a. $0.15 = \dfrac{[2x][x]}{[1-x][x]}$

b. $0.15 = \dfrac{[2x][x]}{[1-x][1-x]}$

c. $0.15 = \dfrac{[2x]^2[x]}{[1-x][1-x]}$

d. $0.15 = \dfrac{[2x][2x]}{[1-x][x]}$

19. Once the reaction has reached equilibrium, which of the following could be done to increase the rate of reaction to the right?

a. Increase the concentration of salt
b. Mix the solution thoroughly
c. Heat the solution
d. Add more magnesium chloride

20. A particular radioactive element emits 2 beta particles and two alpha particles. The atomic mass of this element as a result has decreased by what amount?
    a. 0 amu
    b. 2 amu
    c. 4 amu
    d. 8 amu

21. Given the fact that thorium has a radioactive decay half-life of 14 billion years, which of the following is true?
    a. The earth is only 4.5 billion years old, and as a result, more than half the thorium existing at the formation of the earth still exists today.
    b. Thorium's long half-life is a result of its emission of beta-particles.
    c. Thorium, due to its long half-life, is an easy radioactive element to remove.
    d. None of the above are true.

22. In the following oxidation reduction reaction, what is the balanced half reaction for oxidation?

$$O_3 + H_2O + SO_2 \rightarrow SO_4^{2-} + O_2 + 2H^+$$

    a. $H_2O \rightarrow 2H^+ + 2e^- + O$
    b. $O_3 + SO_2 \rightarrow SO_4^{2-} + O_2$
    c. $H_2O + e^- \rightarrow O_2 + 2H+$
    d. $O_3 + H_2O + SO_2 \rightarrow 2e^-$

23. A battery is a form of a galvanic cell in which species are being oxidized and reduced to generate a current, which can power your cell phone, camera, etc. Which end of a battery is being oxidized when the battery is generating a current?
    a. The positive end
    b. The negative end
    c. The coating of the batter
    d. Both ends perform an oxidizing reaction.

24. A scientist is designing a new type of galvanic cell. He wants the reaction in the galvanic cell to start spontaneously, without any initial input of charge. For this to occur, which of the following must be true?
    a. The net cell potential must be less than zero.
    b. The oxidation potential needs to be greater than the reduction potential.
    c. The reduction potential needs to be greater than the oxidation potential.
    d. The Gibbs free energy of the reaction needs to be positive.

25. Which of the following molecules contains a bond that is ionic?
    a. BF_4
    b. NiO_2
    c. CH_4
    d. O_2

26. Jack has just finished taking his chemistry exam and has named some compounds on a question. Which of these has he named incorrectly?
    I.   LiCl – Lithium chloride
    II. $CuSO_4$ – Copper Sulfite
    III. SiO_2 – Silica trioxide
    IV. PbI_2 – Lead Iodide

    a. I only
    b. II only
    c. II and IV
    d. II and III

Problems 27-29 refer to the information given below.

A student is measuring the heat capacity of an unknown compound. He places 20 grams of the compound onto an insulated hot plate that emits 20 joules of heat per second. After 10 seconds, he finds that the temperature has increased by 45 °C.

Next, he places 5 grams of the compound into a bomb calorimeter, and ignites it. The water surrounding the bomb calorimeter increases in temperature by 8.5 °C.

27. **What is the heat capacity of this compound?**
    a. 2.5 J/g*C
    b. 3.33 J/g*C
    c. 4.44 J/g*C
    d. 5.0 J/g*C

28. **From a calorimetry experiment. The enthalpy of reaction, which is the heat released or consumed, can be determined. What is the enthalpy of reaction for this compound?**
    a. -25.5 kJ/mol
    b. -47.2 kJ/mol
    c. -81.0 kJ/mol
    d. There is not enough information from this experiment to determine the enthalpy of reaction.

29. **Assuming that the unknown compound was a form of hydrocarbon, what are the reaction products that would have been produced in the bomb calorimeter?**
    a. Water and carbon dioxide
    b. Carbon dioxide and carbon monoxide
    c. Carbon dioxide only
    d. Water and methane

30. **Of which group of elements in the periodic table is this statement true of? "These elements are most conductive and can have various ionic charges."**
    a. Alkali earth metals
    b. Transition metals
    c. Halogens
    d. Lanthanides

31. **Ideal gas behavior is just that: behavior of gases in a perfect world. However, in the real world this is not usually the case. Which of these gases would be expected to act the least ideally?**
    a. Water vapor
    b. Ammonia (NH_3)
    c. Nitrogen gas
    d. Helium gas

32. Nitric chloride is a rare compound that is formed according to the reaction below:

$$N_2 + 3\ Cl_2 \rightarrow 2NCl_2 \quad \Delta H = 510\ kJ/mol$$

This reaction occurs in the gas phase. Which of the following statements is true?

    a. This reaction is exothermic.
    b. In order for this reaction to occur, the temperature must be increased dramatically.
    c. This reaction does not occur spontaneously under any conditions.
    d. At room temperature, increasing the concentration of nitrogen gas will significantly speed up the reaction.

33. A 200 mL solution of 0.1 molar sulfuric acid is mixed with a 200 mL solution of 0.2 molar NH_3. What is the approximate pH of the resulting solution?
    a. Between 0 and 1
    b. Between 1 and 3
    c. Between 3 and 7
    d. Greater than 7

34. Which of the following statements about Van der Waal's forces is true?
    a. Hydrogen bonds are a type of Van der Waal's force.
    b. Van der Waal's forces are caused by an electronegativity difference across a bond.
    c. Van der Waal's forces are small intramolecular forces.
    d. Van der Waal's forces can be generated by the interaction of 2 permanent dipoles.

35. **As the rate of hydrogen bonding in a compound increases, which of the following will occur?**
    a. The boiling point will increase
    b. The boiling point will decrease
    c. The melting point will increase
    d. Both A and C will occur.

36. **Peter mixes 15 grams of calcium hydroxide with 30 grams of zinc chloride. What reagent will be the limiting reactant, and approximately how much of the excess reagent is there?**
    a. Calcium hydroxide, 6 grams
    b. Calcium hydroxide, 3 grams
    c. Zinc chloride, 2 grams
    d. Zinc chloride 3.5 grams

37. **Out of the following items, which can be used to identify the pH of a solution?**
    I.   **Methyl orange indicator**
    II.   **Litmus paper**
    III.   **pH probe**

    a. I only
    b. II and III
    c. I and III
    d. I, II, and III

38. **In the laboratory, John finds an unlabeled beaker of material. He needs to find out what it is. To do this, which of the following tests should he perform?**
    a. Adding acid to the beaker.
    b. Sniffing the beaker.
    c. Mixing water into the beaker.
    d. None of the above.

39. The Kc equilibrium constant is:
   a. Always the same as the Kp equilibrium constant.
   b. Derived from the ratio of reactants to products at equilibrium.
   c. Determined empirically.
   d. A constant value of 0.08206

40. In the reaction below, a scientist has determined the equilibrium constant is 1.8×10^{-2}. He increases the temperature of the experiment. What will happen to the equilibrium constant?

$$4 NH_3(g) + 3 O_2(g) \rightarrow 2 N_2(g) + 6 H_2O(g) + energy$$

   a. It will increase
   b. It will decrease
   c. It will remain the same
   d. It will become equal to the reaction quotient for the experiment.

41. What is the correct balanced equation of the reaction below?

$$NH_4NO_3 + heat \rightarrow N_2O + H_2O$$

   a. This equation is already balanced.
   b. $3 NH_4NO_3 + heat \rightarrow 3 N_2O + 2 H_2O$
   c. $2 NH_4NO_3 + heat \rightarrow 2 N_2O + H_2O$
   d. $NH_4NO_3 + heat \rightarrow N_2O + 2 H_2O$

42. In a chemical reaction, the entropy will always increase if:
   a. The enthalpy value of the reaction is positive
   b. The enthalpy value of the reaction is negative
   c. If the number of mols of product exceeds the number of mols of reactant
   d. If the number of mols of reactant exceeds the number of mols of product

43. A student is purifying copper ore (Cu_2O) through a hydration reaction, in which excess H_2 is used to reduce the copper into its natural state. If 0.5 mols of copper ore is consumed in the reaction, how much pure copper will be produced?
    a. 31.2 grams
    b. 63.5 grams
    c. 128.2 grams
    d. None of the above

44. Ethanol (CH_3CH_2OH) is a fuel that can be used in cars, but it has a lower energy density than gasoline (C_8H_{18}). However, the density of the two fuels is about the same. The lower energy obtained from the combustion of ethanol is likely due to:
    a. The hydrogen bonding that exists in the ethanol liquid.
    b. The presence of an oxygen molecule in ethanol.
    c. The greater number of carbon atoms present in ethanol compared to gasoline.
    d. The hydrophilic properties of ethanol.

45. Stephen places 20 grams of salt into a 100 mL solution of benzene (C_6H_6). Approximately how much of the salt will be soluble?
    a. Less than 1 gram
    b. 1-5 grams
    c. 5-10 grams
    d. more than 10 grams

46. What is the concentration of hydroxide anions present in a solution that has a pOH of 5?
    a. 0.001 M
    b. 0.0001 M
    c. 0.00001 M
    d. 0.000001 M

Questions 47 to 48 refer to the information below.

A scientist has determined that he wants to use zinc as one half reaction in a galvanic cell. This reaction is:

$$Zn^{2+} + 2\ e^- \rightarrow Zn(s) \qquad E = -0.76\ V.$$

Below is a table of other half reactions that could be paired in this galvanic cell.

$Ag^+(aq) + e^- \rightarrow Ag(s)$	0.80
$Fe^{3+}(aq) + e^- \rightarrow Fe^{2+}(aq)$	0.77
$Co^{3+}(aq) + e^- \rightarrow Co^{2+}(aq)$	1.82

47. Which metal would be most favorable to use in pairing with the zinc half reaction?
    a. Silver
    b. Iron
    c. Cobalt
    d. Zinc

48. What is the cell potential of the galvanic cell if the half reaction used is: $Cu^{2+}(aq) + 2e^- \rightarrow Cu(s)$, E = 0.34?
    a. 0.34
    b. 0.42
    c. 1.10
    d. 1.44

49. **Which of the following elements will have a first ionization energy that is greater than that of oxygen?**
    a. Fluorine
    b. Lithium
    c. Calcium
    d. Carbon

50. **Which of the following charts below shows the reaction rate as a function of concentration for a reactant with a reaction order of 2?**

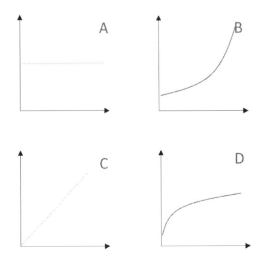

    a. A
    b. B
    c. C
    d. D

51. **In a calorimeter, what is measured to determine the specific enthalpy of a reaction?**
    a. The concentration of products formed.
    b. The temperature of water in the calorimeter.
    c. The temperature of air outside the calorimeter.
    d. The rate of reaction of the reagents.

52. **At 0 °C, water can exist as both a solid and a liquid, although that temperature is the freezing point of water. In order for all the water to become liquid, which of the following must happen?**

a. Intramolecular bonds between water molecules need to be broken.
b. Hydrogen bonds between water molecules needs to be broken.
c. Acid needs to be added to the water to reduce the pH.
d. The activation energy of the phase change from solid to liquid needs to be reduced.

53. Which of the following is true about a chemical reaction that results in zero change in entropy?
a. The reaction enthalpy must have been zero as well.
b. The Gibbs free energy change must have been zero as well.
c. There was no reaction.
d. The temperature change in the reaction must have been zero.

54. According to Le Chatelier's principle, if we add products to the reaction seen below, what will happen?

$$BaCl_2 \text{ (aq)} + H_2SO_4 \text{ (aq)} \rightarrow BaSO_4 \text{ (s)} + 2 \text{ HCl (aq)}$$

a. The reaction will shift to the left, and more reagents will be formed.
b. The reaction will shift to the right, and more products will be formed.
c. If the reaction is exothermic, the reaction will shift to the left. If the reaction is endothermic, the reaction will shift to the right.
d. Nothing will happen to this reaction.

55. If we mix 100 mL of a 0.1 molar solution of HCl, which has a pH of 1.8, with a 100 mL solution of 0.2 molar HCl, which of the following will occur?
a. The pH will remain the same
b. The pH will decrease slightly
c. The pH will increase slightly
d. The pH will be neutralized at 7.

56. **A student is preparing an eluent solution for ion chromatography, which needs to be exactly 50 mM NaOH. To prepare a 1 liter solution of this, he should:**
    a. Add 2 grams of NaOH to a 2 liter Erlenmeyer flask, and fill to the 1 liter mark.
    b. Add 4 grams of NaOH to a 1 liter beaker, and fill to the 1 liter mark.
    c. Add 2 grams of NaOH to a 1 liter volumetric flask, and fill to the 1 liter mark.
    d. Add 4 grams of NaOH to a 2 liter graduated cylinder, and fill to the 1 liter mark.

57. **In an enclosed container of gas, the pressure on the walls of the gas is exerted due to the:**
    a. Intermolecular forces of the gas
    b. The collision of gas molecules with the walls of the container
    c. The electronic repulsion of gas molecules away from each other
    d. The speed of the gas molecules

58. **Covalent bonds are formed due to the sharing of an electron pair between two atoms. In which of these processes below is a covalent bond actually broken?**
    a. Gold (Au) melts
    b. Silver nitrate dissociates into water
    c. Solid carbon is heated to a high temperature and sublimates
    d. Fructose is dissolved into water.

59. **In an acid base titration, the equivalence point can be determined through the use of a colorimetric additive. In a redox titration, how can we tell when electrons are no longer being transferred, at which point the redox equivalence point has been reached?**
    a. Using a potentiometer
    b. Using a pH meter
    c. Using phenolphthalein as an indicator
    d. None of the above will work for a redox titration

60. In a combustion reaction, carbon dioxide is produced. A student wants to measure the extent of reaction for a combustion reaction in a laboratory. To do this, the carbon dioxide is cooled over water, and then collected. However, she finds that the carbon dioxide mass collected does not match with the amount of reagent combusted. A possible explanation for this is that:

    a. The carbon dioxide was further combusted into carbon ash and oxygen gas.
    b. The carbon dioxide became dissolved into the cooling water.
    c. Carbon dioxide is not a major product of a combustion reaction and is produced in too small quantities to measure.
    d. Carbon dioxide reacted with water to form carbon monoxide and OH-.

Free Response Questions

There are four short response questions, which should be answered in approximately paragraph with any associated diagrams, and three long response questions.

Long Response:

1. In water, hydrochloric acid will dissociate to form hydronium ions and chlorine ions, according to the equation below:

$$HCl + H_2O \rightarrow H_3O^+ + Cl^-$$

The K_a for this reaction is 5.4×10^{-4}.

a. What is the equilibrium-constant equation for this dissociation reaction?

b. If 0.25 mols of hydrochloric acid are placed into 1 liter of water, what is the pH of the solution?

c. Using hydrochloric acid, is it possible to form a buffer solution? If so, use the Hendersen-Hasselbach equation to demonstrate the pH at which a buffer solution could exist. If not, explain why not.

2. The table below presents the enthalpy of formation of several common compounds

Compound	H_f (kJ/mol)
NH_3	-80.8
N_2	0
CH_4	-74.8
$NaHCO_3$	-950.8

a. Why does nitrogen have an enthalpy of formation value of 0?

b. Write the balanced equations for the formation of ammonia, methane, and sodium bicarbonate.

c. Which of the compounds in the table, other than nitrogen, is the most likely to form spontaneously at room temperature, assuming all reactants are present?

3. A student is performing a titration on a weak acid, HCN with a strong base, NaOH.

    a. Draw a predicted titration chart for this experiment.

    b. How would this titration chart look different if instead the student was titrating phosphoric acid, H_3PO_4?

    c. Based on the titration curve seen below, what is the pKa of the unknown acid? Explain your analysis.

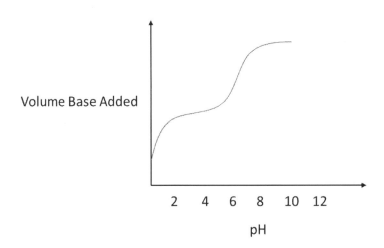

Short Response:

4. Write the balanced chemical reaction equations for any 3 of the 5 reactions described below. Additionally, describe the reaction type (i.e. synthesis, decomposition, etc.).

    a. A solution of hydrochloric acid is mixed with a solution of calcium hydroxide.

    b. A piece of solid zinc is placed into a solution of hydrochloric acid.

    c. Methane (natural gas) is combusted.

    d. A solution of sodium chloride is mixed with a solution of silver nitrate.

    e. Hydrogen and nitrogen gas are heated at elevated temperature and pressure.

5. A student is given three compounds to identify. It is known that the compounds are Al_2O_3, $NaHCO_3$, and $MgCrO_4$. The student uses several experiments to try and identify the substances, labeled A, B, and C. The data the student obtains is seen below.

Compound	Solubility in water	pH in pure water	Reaction with HCl
A	32g/L	8.2	Yes, bubbles
B	Negligible	n/a	Yes
C	96g/L	6.2	Yes, foamy

a. Based on this information, what is the identity of each compound and why?

b. Write a chemical equation that shows the dissociation of compound C in water, demonstrating its acidity.

c. The compounds given in this question are relatively different. How would you distinguish two compounds that are very similar, for example Na_2CO3 and $NaHCO_3$?

6. Identify the VSEPR geometry of the four compounds listed below:

$$CH_4 \qquad NH_3 \qquad H_2PO_4^{-} \qquad SO_2$$

    a. Although sulfate (SO_4) and ammonium (NH_4^{+}) have the same number of ligands, their VSEPR geometry is different. What is the VSEPR geometry of each compound and why are they different?

    b. Indicate whether or not you agree with the statement below, and support your answer:

    "The number of bonds an element can form is directly related to its steric number."

7. A kinetic experiment performed by Clarice results in the data gathered below. The reaction has the general form:

$$A + B \rightarrow C$$

Experiment	[A]	[B]	Initial Rate mol/(L*s)
1	0.15 M	0.08 M	0.162
2	0.29 M	0.085 M	0.324
3	0.14 M	0.16 M	0.648

    a. What is the order of reaction for each reactant, A, and B?

    b. Write the overall rate law equation for this reaction, and state the order of the reaction.

    c. If a reaction is irreversible, does this affect the rate law for the reaction? Explain your reasoning.

Multiple Choice Answers

1.	C	31.	A
2.	D	32.	B
3.	C	33.	B
4.	A	34.	D
5.	B	35.	D
6.	D	36.	B
7.	D	37.	D
8.	B	38.	D
9.	D	39.	B
10.	B	40.	A
11.	B	41.	D
12.	C	42.	C
13.	D	43.	B
14.	C	44.	B
15.	C	45.	A
16.	B	46.	C
17.	A	47.	C
18.	C	48.	C
19.	D	49.	D
20.	D	50.	B
21.	A	51.	B
22.	A	52.	B
23.	B	53.	C
24.	B	54.	D
25.	B	55.	B
26.	D	56.	C
27.	C	57.	B
28.	D	58.	C
29.	A	59.	A
30.	B	60.	B

Free Response Answers

1. This question tests the student on acid base reactions and constants.

   a. The Ka is given, and the reaction can be set up as:

   $$Ka = [H3O+][Cl-]/[HCl][H2O]$$

   The student should mention that all species are reacting and are included in the equation.

   b. Hydrochloric acid is a strong acid. This must be mentioned. Thus, it will dissociate completely. As a result, this will form a 0.25 molarity solution of hydronium ions.

   $$pH = -log(H+) = 0.60$$

   This is a very low pH and the student should discuss that this is extremely acid, since the pH scale goes from 0-14.

   c. Yes! It is possible to form a buffer with a monoprotic acid. However, strong acids can only form buffers at low pH!.

   $$pKa = -log(Ka).$$ The student can calculate this, and find that pKa is 3.26. This means that a buffer can be formed near the pKa point of 3.26.

2. This tests the students' knowledge of heats of reaction.
   a. The enthalpy of formation of pure elements is always zero.
   b. The full equations will not be written out here. However, for a formation reaction, the reactants should always be pure elements, and the products will be the compound. For example:

   $$C + 2H_2 \rightarrow CH_4$$

c. The student needs to discuss the concept of enthalpy, and the meaning of the negative sign. A positive sign means energy is consumed, and a negative sign means energy is released. The more energy released, the more favorable a reaction is, because the end product is more stable. As a result, the chemical with the greatest negative value of Hf will form the most spontaneously, in this case sodium bicarbonate.

3. This tests the student's knowledge of titration.
    a. The titration chart should look like:

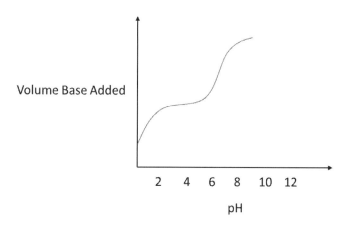

Key elements:

- There can only be one equivalence point (steep slope) seen around pH 7-8.
- The half equivalence point **must** be lower than 7, because this is an acid.
- The graph must have labeled axes.

    b. Phosphoric acid has 3 acidic protons, and as such would have three bends in the chart. Bonus points if the student draws an additional chart to depict this.

    c. The pKa can be found at the half equivalence point, which can be estimated to be around 3.6, as seen below:

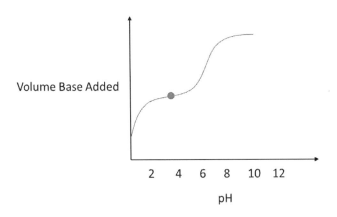

Volume Base Added

2   4   6   8   10 12

pH

4. This is a relatively simply problem. The student can pick any three of the reactions and write the correct, balanced equation. They should give a short rationale for their choosing of the reaction type. They are given below:

    a. $2 HCl + Ca(OH)_2 \rightarrow CaCl_2 + 2 H_2O$ – Acid base reaction
    b. $Zn + 2HCl \rightarrow ZnCl_2 + 2H+$ - Single Replacement reaction
    c. $CH4 + 2 O_2 \rightarrow CO2 + 2 H2O$ – Combustion reaction
    d. $2NaCl + Ag(NO_3)_2 \rightarrow AgCl_2 + 2 NaNO3$ – double displacement, precipitate is formed!
    e. $3 H_2 + N_2 \rightarrow 2 NH_3$ – synthesis

5. This tests a student's understanding of chemical properties and critical thinking in identifying compounds.
    a. The insoluble compound is aluminum oxide.
        i.   Compound C is likely sodium bicarbonate, which has a single acidic proton. Magnesium chromate is not acidic.
        ii. This leaves compound A to be magnesium chromate, which is slightly basic due to the chromate ion's ability to receive a pair of electrons.
    b. Compound C is sodium bicarbonate and will dissociate according to:
        i. $NaHCO3 + H2O \rightarrow Na^+ + H_3O^+ + CO_3^{2-}$
    c. We can identify these two compounds using titration and looking at the curve generated. Na2CO3 is not acidic, and will not generate a standard titration curve. Other methods, such as measuring pH, or spectroscopy, can be accepted, as long as the student adequately explains their use.

6. This tests VSEPR geometry and bonding knowledge.

CH4 is tetrahedral

NH3 is trigonal pyramidal

H_2PO_4 is pentagonal pyramidal

SO2 is bent

    a. The core reason their VSEPR geometry is different is due to the number of free electrons.

    b. This statement correct. The steric number is the number of atoms bonded to the central atom in a molecule, and is thus directly related to the number of bonds an element can form.

7. This question tests understanding of rate law and reaction kinetics.

    a. The student should explain that a linear increase in reaction rate results in a reaction order of 1. An exponential increase is a reaction rate of 2. Thus, A has a reaction order of 1 and B has an order of 2, since increasing the amount of B by X results in a 4X increase in reaction rate.

    b. The overall rate law is: rate = $k[A][B]^2$ The order of the reaction is 3, and is equal to the sum of all the exponents in the rate law equation.

    c. The rate law does not take into account the products, as seen from the standard rate law equation. As a result, the irreversibility of the reaction does not affect the rate law.

Image Sources

1. Original Image

2. Original Image

3. Public Domain
- http://commons.wikimedia.org/wiki/File:Periodic_table.vg

4. Original Image

5. Original Image

6. Original Image

7. Original Image

8. Original Image

9. Original Image

10. Original Image

11. Public Domain
- http://www.public-domain-content.com/encyclopedia/Chemistry/Electronegativity.shtml

12. Original Image

13. Original Image

14. Original Image

15. Public Domain
- http://commons.wikimedia.org/wiki/File:N-Pentan.png

16. Public Domain
- http://commons.wikimedia.org/wiki/File:Isobutanol.png

17. Public Domain
- http://en.wikipedia.org/wiki/File:Phenylalanin_-_Phenylalanine.svg

18. Public Domain
- http://en.wikipedia.org/wiki/File:Fexofenadine.svg

19. Public Domain
- http://en.wikipedia.org/wiki/File:2-amino-pentane.png

20. Public Domain
- http://en.wikipedia.org/wiki/File:Methylamine.png

21. Public Domain
- http://en.wikipedia.org/wiki/File:Formic_acid.svg

22. Public Domain
- http://en.wikipedia.org/wiki/File:Oxals%C3%A4ure3.svg

23. Public Domain
- http://en.wikipedia.org/wiki/File:Fadrozole.png

24. Public Domain
- http://en.wikipedia.org/wiki/File:Letrozole.svg

25. Original Image

26. Original Image

27. Original Image

28. Original Image

29. Original Image

30. Original Image

31. Public Domain
- http://commons.wikimedia.org/wiki/File:Isooctane.png

32. Public Domain
- http://en.wikipedia.org/wiki/File:OctaneFull.png

33. Original Image

34. Original Image

35. Original Image

36. Original Image

37. Original Image

38. Original Image

39. Original Image

40. Original Image

41. Original Image

42. Original Image

43. Original Image

44. Original Image

45. Original Image

46. Public Domain
- http://en.wikipedia.org/wiki/File:Zitronens%C3%A4ure_-_Citric_acid.svg

Made in the USA
San Bernardino, CA
26 August 2014